"'Who am I and what will I do to be who I want to be?' *Safety Skills for Asperger Women* is a powerful invitation to take a chance on life and on healing. At times gentle in its encouragement, at others urging in its counsel, Holliday Willey's words are a beacon, a light in the dark for all women with AS who want to live life more fully but sometimes find themselves off the path. Her work is remarkable, courageous and welcoming for a group of women who too often live lives misunderstood and mistreated. *Safety Skills* is an eye-opening account of the perils and also the victories of the female life on the spectrum. Beautifully written and powerful in its message of wellness, this book helps you to dance with your spirit when life feels too overwhelming."

—*Shana Nichols, Owner and Director of the ASPIRE Center for Learning and Development and author of* Girls Growing Up on the Autism Spectrum

"Liane writes of the agonies she has faced as she traveled the social world full of hazards. Some of the accounts are almost too scary to contemplate, yet her constant optimism has brought her through. Her deep introspection brings us all closer to understanding how an autistic mind experiences the world. She provides end of chapter support sections giving her ideas of things that she feels would be helpful to know. It is clear she hopes others may not have to face similar situations or ordeals unprepared. Liane longs for a world where AS is totally accepted; it is writ large on every page. It would address the extreme stresses many have to live with on a daily basis. Liane's book could help vulnerable women with AS live a safer, happier life."

—*Rosalyn Lord, parent, advocate and trainer, UK*

"In the chapter titled 'Out and About: Or Traveling To and Fro,' Liane Holliday Willey describes several challenging travel adventures—across the continent and around the block—in vivid Aspie detail. The wording of an informational sign at an airport, confusing pronunciations of her name over an airport loudspeaker, the resultant stressful interaction with an airline representative, rearranged shelves in grocery stores that set off the routine-bound author in a bad way, all illustrate sensory and social situations that could make travel daunting, difficult and something to avoid for many living on the spectrum. Yet, Liane understands that the basic human desire to explore the world and the benefits of doing so,

however difficult it may be, outweigh the dilemmas. This chapter alone makes *Safety Skills for Asperger Women* a must-read!"
—*Dennis Debbaudt, founder of Autism Risk & Safety Management and author of* Autism, Advocates and Law Enforcement Professionals

"Liane's wise and intimate account of how to recognize, disarm and distance oneself from those who might intend or not emotional or social harm connected with me in ways I couldn't have otherwise imagined… Liane's book is totally enthralling…it opened doors for me to explanations of past events as well as explaining how to move my life forward with confidence and self-assurance. It left a taste of 'up and at 'em girl' upon my pallet and I'm most grateful to Liane for having written such an insightful and empowering account that can equip me to deal with past and future events; especially with ideas of keeping my emotions and heart safe!"
—*Wendy Lawson, psychologist, qualified counselor, social worker, autism advocate and author of many books on topics relating to autism spectrum disorders*

"The literary equivalent of a map, a first aid kit, a bullet proof vest and a nice cup of tea. Liane's strength is not the stoic sort, but shows itself through vulnerability, honesty and generosity. This is on the top shelf of 'must reads' in the category of female Asperger syndrome and it shall remain there to arm, console and inform readers for many years to come!"
—*Rudy Simone, author of* Aspergirls *and* 22 Things a Woman Must Know: If She Loves a Man with Asperger's Syndrome

"Liane Holliday Willey's book will help many women on the autism spectrum have a more fulfilling life."
—*Temple Grandin, author of* Thinking in Pictures *and* The Way I See It

Safety *Skills*

FOR

Asperger
Women

by the same author

Pretending to be Normal
Living with Asperger's Syndrome
Liane Holliday Willey
Foreword by Tony Attwood
ISBN 978 1 85302 749 9

Asperger Syndrome in the Family
Redefining Normal
Liane Holliday Willey
Foreword by Pamela B. Tanguay
ISBN 978 1 85302 873 1

Asperger Syndrome in Adolescence
Living with the Ups, the Downs and Things in Between
Edited by Liane Holliday Willey
Foreword by Luke Jackson
ISBN 978 1 84310 742 2

of related interest

The Complete Guide to Asperger's Syndrome
Tony Attwood
ISBN 978 1 84310 669 2

Aspergirls
Empowering Females with Asperger Syndrome
Rudy Simone
Foreword by Liane Holliday Willey
ISBN 978 1 84905 826 1

Safety *Skills*

FOR

Asperger Women

HOW TO SAVE

A PERFECTLY

GOOD FEMALE LIFE

LIANE HOLLIDAY WILLEY, EdD

FOREWORD BY TONY ATTWOOD

Jessica Kingsley *Publishers*
London and Philadelphia

First published in 2012
by Jessica Kingsley Publishers
116 Pentonville Road
London N1 9JB, UK
and
400 Market Street, Suite 400
Philadelphia, PA 19106, USA

www.jkp.com

Library of Congress Cataloging in Publication Data
Willey, Liane Holliday.
Safety skills for asperger women : how to save a perfectly good female life
/ Liane Holliday Willey ; foreword by Tony Attwood.
p. cm.
Includes bibliographical references.
ISBN 978-1-84905-836-0 (alk. paper)
1. Willey, Liane Holliday--Health. 2. Asperger's syndrome--Patients--
Biography. 3. Asperger's syndrome--Popular works. I. Title.
RC553.A88W565 2011
616.85'8832--dc22
2011007368

British Library Cataloguing in Publication Data
A CIP catalogue record for this book is available from the British Library

ISBN 9781849058360

Printed and bound in the United States

*Without my parents, this book would not have been written.
Thanks to my mother for helping me learn the NT dance.
Thanks to my father for showing me who I am.*

Acknowledgments

To all the ladies and the gentleman who were gracious enough to write introductions to each of the chapters: The work you do to support people with ASD and the friendship you have shared with me are priceless. Thank you for all you do!

To all the people who share a passion for sending the ASD female message forward: Applause, applause, applause. Standing ovation for you all!

To Jessica Kingsley: Your books continue to serve as the standard best titles we have in ASD research, theory and practice. Speaking on behalf of all your readers, thank you!!!

To my daughters: Thank you my loves, for all the support and encouragement you give to me and to others on the spectrum. Your efforts behind the scenes of my work is worth the world to me. You each amaze me everyday with your insight and intelligence.

Contents

Foreword

This was not an easy book for Liane to write. As I read the manuscript for *Safety Skills for Asperger Women,* I could hear Liane's voice and feel compassion for my friend as she described her experiences as a girl, woman and mother that included moments of vulnerability, despair, confusion and self-doubt. Clinicians tend to focus on the positive attributes of having Asperger's syndrome, and there are many; but there are also less positive aspects that need to be known, described by Liane as "the scary stuff," in order to, in Liane's subtitle for this book, *save a perfectly good female life.* Her personal explanations and advice will resonate with the reader and transform and even save lives.

Why is this book so needed and so valuable? Primarily, because our understanding of Asperger's syndrome is based on the profile of abilities and developmental history of boys and men. Their adaptations and behaviour can be quite conspicuous and, as the male to female ratio for Asperger's syndrome is 4:1, clinicians will have greater experience identifying the male expression and reaction to the diagnostic characteristics. Girls and women who have Asperger's syndrome are different, not in terms of the core characteristics, but in terms of their reaction to being different. They use specific coping and adjustment strategies to camouflage or mask their confusion in social situations, and may achieve superficial social success by imitation or escaping into a world of fantasy or nature. Clinicians need a paradigm shift in terms of their recognition of the female presentation of Asperger's syndrome to ensure earlier diagnosis and access to effective understanding and support. Liane's new book enables greater recognition of the adversity experienced by girls and women who have Asperger's syndrome, and provides strategies to overcome or avoid "scary" moments.

In early childhood, probably long before a diagnostic assessment, a girl who has the characteristics of Asperger's syndrome will begin to know she is different to other girls. She may not identify with or want to play cooperatively with her female peers. She may consider that the play of other girls is stupid, boring and inexplicable, and prefer to play alone so that she can do things her own way. Her interests can be different to other girls', not necessarily in terms of focus, but intensity and quality. There may be a determination to organize toys rather than share them, and also not play with toys in conventional ways. For example, she may collect over 50 Barbie dolls yet choose not to enact with her neighbourhood friends "Barbie getting married," but instead arrange the dolls in particular configurations. She may prefer non-gender specific toys such as Lego, and not seek acquisitions related to the latest craze for girls her age in order to be "cool" and popular. She may be averse to the concept of femininity, choosing not to wear the latest fashions or fancy or frilly clothing. Her preference may be for practical, comfortable clothing with lots of pockets. While boys with Asperger's syndrome may fixate on facts (and some girls with Asperger's syndrome can also have an encyclopaedic knowledge of specific topics), many girls have an intense interest in reading and escaping into fiction, enjoying a fantasy world, creating a new persona, talking to imaginary friends and writing fiction at an early age. Another escape for girls with Asperger's syndrome is into the exciting world of nature, as many have an intuitive understanding of animals rather than people. Animals are safe; they are loyal, enthusiastic and appreciative friends who never tease or reject their owners.

If she does have friendships, they are likely to be quite intense and with one other girl, who may provide guidance for her in social situations. In return, the girl with Asperger's syndrome is a loyal and helpful friend, rarely interested in the "bitchy" behaviour of her peers. Unfortunately, sometimes the girl who has Asperger's syndrome is vulnerable to friendship predators who take advantage of her naivety, social immaturity and desperation for a friend. Since it is inevitable that there will be times when she has to engage with other children, she may well prefer to play with boys, whose play is more constructive and adventurous rather than emotional and conversational. Many girls and women who have Asperger's syndrome have described to clinicians and in autobiographies how they sometimes think they have a male rather than a female brain, having a greater understanding and appreciation of the interests, thinking and humour of boys. The girl who has Asperger's syndrome may be described as a tomboy, eager to join in the activities and conversations of boys rather than girls.

When boys who have Asperger's syndrome make a social error, their response may be to become agitated. Their clumsy and immature social play skills are quite conspicuous and annoying to both peers and adults. There is clear recognition that this child needs an assessment and intervention. Girls, on the other hand, are more likely to apologize and appease when making a social error. Peers and adults may then forgive and forget, but without realizing that a pattern is emerging. However, the girl with Asperger's syndrome is increasingly recognizing her own social confusion and frequent faux pas. She may react by trying to stay on the periphery of social situations, and not be noticed in a group, so that others remain unaware of her social confusion. She may be an avid observer of human behaviour, trying to decipher what she is supposed to do or say. Another strategy she may use to counter her difficulties with social reasoning is to be well behaved and compliant at school so as not to be noticed or recognized as different. A girl with Asperger's syndrome may suffer her social confusion in silence and isolation in the classroom or playground, yet be a very different character at home. The "mask" is removed, and she may use passive-aggressive behaviour to control her family and social experiences.

Another, more constructive, adaptation to the characteristics of Asperger's syndrome used by girls and women is to engage in imitation or imagination. The girl may identify someone who is socially successful and popular, either a peer or a character in a television soap opera, and adopt that person's persona by mimicking speech patterns, phrases, body language and even clothing and interests. She becomes someone else, someone who would be accepted and not recognized as different. She learns how to act in specific situations, a strategy that Liane found so successful that people thought her social abilities were intuitive, and could not believe this was a performance. Girls and women who have Asperger's syndrome can be like chameleons, changing personas according to the situation, with no one knowing the genuine person. They believe that the real person must remain secret because they fear that person is defective.

Some girls may not seek integration, but instead escape into imagination. A girl may feel that if she cannot be successful with her peers, she can try to find an alternative world where she is valued and appreciated. She may identify with a fictional character such as Harry Potter or Hermione Granger, who face adversity but have special powers and friends. If she feels lonely, then imaginary friends can provide companionship, support and comfort. Alternatively, she may develop an interest in ancient civilizations to find an old world where she could perhaps feel at home; or a fascination with another country, such as Japan, where she might be accepted and among people of like mind. She may develop an interest in science fiction, imagining herself belonging on another planet; or a special and intense interest in the traditional fantasy worlds of witches, fairies and mythology. Many typical children occasionally enjoy escaping into imagination, but for the girl with Asperger's syndrome, the reasons are qualitatively different. The fantasy world becomes a means of avoiding reality and experiencing a relatively safe and successful social life.

These coping and camouflaging mechanisms may mask the characteristics of Asperger's syndrome for some time, such that the girl slips through the diagnostic net. However, there is a psychological cost that may only become apparent in adolescence. It is emotionally exhausting to be constantly observing and analyzing social behaviour, and trying not to make a social error; adopting an alternative persona can lead to confusion with self-identity and low self-esteem. Both of these coping and camouflaging strategies can contribute to a clinical depression in a young adult. Girls and women who have Asperger's syndrome can spend many years searching for an explanation of why they are different, questioning whether they are defective or demented and why they feel so depressed.

In the girl's attempt to mask her social confusion and cope with her anxiety, she may be vulnerable to a range of social difficulties and psychological disorders. In many instances, her behaviour is misinterpreted, potentially leading to misdiagnosis. For example, her excessive social anxiety may lead to selective mutism, where she is unable to speak at all in a group situation. Some girls with Asperger's syndrome develop rigid routines, rituals and special interests to alleviate anxiety. If these rituals and interests revolve around food, calories and nutrition, especially during adolescence when stress may be increased, they may develop signs of Anorexia Nervosa or Bulimia.

According to several autobiographies (and from my own extensive clinical experience), women who have Asperger's syndrome can be extremely sensitive to the emotional atmosphere at social gatherings. There can be an almost "sixth sense" for others' feelings of antagonism, fear and despair. This hypersensitivity to negative emotions, combined with the woman's own experiences of bullying, rejection and betrayal, can lead to her behaving in a way that is suggestive of borderline personality disorder.

For some girls and women with Asperger's syndrome there may be sexual issues. For example, a tendency to be a tomboy in childhood, a subsequent rejection of the symbols of femininity, such as fashion, make-up and perfumes, and an appreciation of the logic of the male brain can lead to concerns regarding sexual orientation and gender identity. In addition, the girl's social immaturity and naivety can render her vulnerable to sexual predators and the risk of sexual abuse.

Liane used imitation to become socially successful, described eloquently in her autobiography *Pretending to be Normal*. This strategy can, unfortunately, lead clinicians to suspect characteristics of multiple personality disorder, while an escape into a fantasy world and imaginary companions can have clinicians suspecting that signs of schizophrenia could be developing in an adolescent girl with Asperger's syndrome. Equally, her possession of a very sensitive sensory system (for example hearing sounds inaudible to others, and an emotional "sixth sense") can lead to an interest in the supernatural, which could also be misinterpreted as a sign of not being in touch with reality.

Thus, an adolescent or young woman with Asperger's syndrome may only come to the attention of clinicians for the diagnostic assessment of a secondary mood or personality disorder, or psychosis. A detailed developmental history by a clinician experienced in the clinical presentation of adolescent girls with Asperger's syndrome may confirm the characteristics of Asperger's syndrome. At last, an accurate diagnosis and explanation, but she may have missed the opportunity for crucial understanding, guidance and support in her earlier childhood.

Liane wrote one of the first autobiographies, *Pretending to be Normal*, and she has now written one of the first books to describe how to understand and help a girl or woman who has Asperger's syndrome. She "figured out how to play the neurotypical game." It was not easy and there were scary moments, but we need to know about those moments and listen to her wisdom in order to reduce the likelihood of other girls and women having the same ordeals. Her experiences and abilities changed with maturity, and she now has insight, perspective and constructive coping strategies that will be greatly appreciated not only by girls and women who have Asperger's syndrome, but also by all those who support and love them.

Tony Attwood
Minds and Hearts Clinic, Brisbane, Australia
March 2011

Introduction

Like many women over 30ish, I was diagnosed with Asperger syndrome (AS) after my young daughter received her official diagnosis. My father was diagnosed soon after that. My young cousin received her diagnosis when she was four. Clearly, my family carries the autism gene. Of the four of us, three have AS. My father and I would never have been diagnosed with an autism spectrum disorder (ASD) had it not been for my daughter's diagnostic team at Kansas University who suggested I should seek a diagnosis too. Dr. Tony Attwood, a practicing clinical psychologist, best-selling author on the subject and world-renowned pioneer on AS, became the first expert to diagnose me. Over the years, three other psychologists and one psychiatrist joined in and told me I had ASD. I was seeing one of the psychologists for marriage counseling; after I had taken a series of tests and spent many hours in his office discussing my childhood and current thoughts and mind processes, he asked me in a very somber tone if anyone had ever mentioned I might have autistic-like tendencies. I had to laugh and then explain I had Asperger syndrome. It seems that sooner or later my ASD reveals itself, and for that I am happy. I wouldn't have said this a few decades ago. For a while, I kept insisting I could not possibly have AS because the folks I met who were on the cusp of this new diagnosis called Asperger syndrome, seemed to deal with more complex issues than I did. Turns out years of trial and error and immense support from my parents, friends, teachers and physicians had taught me how to cover up, cope with, and compensate for my differences. I was 37 when I sought a diagnosis. By then, I had figured out how to play the neurotypical game. Kind of.

Once I received confirmation that there were others who had to go through the same thinking maze I did just to figure out a joke, and other people who got physically ill after spending a tiny amount of time at a social gathering, and people who wore ear plugs and people who struggled with simple things like catching a ball or tying their shoes, and so on through the Aspie way, I felt a warming toward wholeness. With the discovery of others like me, I could finally see the hairline cracks in the window between the me society saw, and the me I knew.

Looking back, it was idealistic of me to think I could let the real me out without giving fair warning to the people who only saw me when I was pretending to be normal, but discovering AS was like finding a treasure too lovely to hide. I flew my Aspie flag high and wide, literally flapping with happiness, telling everyone all about my Aspie diagnosis. I was so happy in those first few days of discovery. Then my heart fell.

I believe people feel fear or experience disbelief when they are given information that contradicts what they think they know. I think that happens to people with ASD all the time. I should have known it would be the same for my neurotypical acquaintances. What I could not have predicted were the looks that seemed to say to me *lady, you're crazy* when I started to make my first attempts at disclosure. Sure, my disclosure methods were jumbly and not very polished, but they were honest and true. I didn't put a whole lot of wow factor behind the discovery because it fit so well. To me it was like making a no big deal announcement akin to something like saying I really had dark hair, after having lightened it for so many years. My disclosure went something like this: *Hey, it's not rocket science, but it turns out my brain works differently from most people. You see, this guy named Hans Asperger discovered there were people who acted with many autism-like traits, but in many ways they were different. They were more verbal and had higher IQs. Named after Hans, people like me have a neurobiological make up that scientists and doctors call Asperger syndrome. Isn't that interesting! Doesn't that explain so much about my eccentricities? Cool!*

That's pretty much what I said to people. A fast course in ASD presented on a no-big-deal plate. I didn't suspect my disclosure would plop like a broken egg out of a nest. But even if I had a chance to retell my story over again, I doubt I would change much. I'm not sure I have the patience I would need to plan a well-orchestrated coming-out party. I can give pretty solid advice on disclosure, but when it comes to my own life, I just spill the beans. In this case, my spilled beans did not grow up to be an awesome life-affirming stalk worthy of a giant's attention. Flat-out telling my associates and peers about Aspie Liane may have given people the nudge they needed to disregard me and it may have left me wondering if I would ever have what it takes to make and keep a pal, but that's just one side to the story. To every negative there is a positive, and the positive of my story is this: When I unveiled my differences out loud and for real, I could start to work through years of bad memories, discomfort, abuse, confusion, depression, anxiety and poor self-esteem. What a relief. More than that—what an awesome opportunity to really think about acting within life, rather than reacting to life.

Society is changing for everyone, not just for people with AS. Gender roles are shifting, with more females becoming real players in politics and finance, and more males sharing the duties of home and hearth. The generation gap is closing now that technology and the media are giving all ages the opportunity to share each other's schema. Cultural biases are certainly still struggling to hang on, but even they are eroding at a faster pace than ever before. The more we share the more we learn about one another. So too is it for people like me. As a culture, people with AS are shining a light on the benefits of originality, including our way of thinking and seeing the world. We are forming groups and powerful organizations all over the world to ask for equal rights and to showcase the value of being Aspie. These are obviously all-good things. But in our eagerness to promote all we are capable of and all we can add to the world, we sometimes forget our differences will always make interactions complex, challenging and, at times, simply unsafe.

As a woman on the spectrum, I am well acquainted with the thorns that cut us until we bleed. In addition to the typical hurdles put in our way by ASD, there are a variety of ominous scenarios females are particularly susceptible to. I have walked smack into many of those bad places. I have come face-to-face with some cruel people. Unfortunately, I am not alone.

Over the years, women from all over the globe have shared stories with me about their individual struggles and challenges. Because we are still living in a world where research states males are four times more likely to have AS than are females, it remains difficult for women, particularly adult women, to get a proper diagnosis of AS and the support systems that would follow. As a result, women with an ASD diagnosis are banding together to help other women on the spectrum find their way through the ominous jungle society is so slow to help us cut through. Thankfully, we are not completely alone in our journey. There is a select group of researchers and clinicians who are devoted to changing the way the clinical world defines AS in women. Among our staunchest advocates is Dr. Shana Nichols, who succinctly sums up the AS/female conundrum in a discussion she and I had not too long ago, saying:

Females with ASDs often develop "coping mechanisms" that can cover up the intrinsic difficulties they experience. They may mimic their peers, watch from the sidelines, use their intellect to figure out the best ways to remain undetected, and they will study, practice and learn appropriate approaches to social situations. Sounds easy enough, but in fact these strategies take a lot of work and can more often than not lead to exhaustion, withdrawal, anxiety, selective mutism and depression.

It is clear women with ASD are different from men on the spectrum. It is also clear we are particularly vulnerable to a host of physical and neurobiological challenges that, if left unattended to, will surely devastate who we are. That's where this book comes in.

In my first book *Pretending to be Normal: Living with Asperger's Syndrome*, I wrote about my life's adventure with AS. My intent was to shed light on the diagnosis, which was still rather new to health professionals and the world. I spoke from my own experiences and made no claim that what I felt and dealt with would be the same things other people had to manage. I remain humbly surprised and incredibly touched by the number of people who have written to tell me my words echo their thoughts. The positive affirmation from people I will likely never meet in person has made me feel special and genuinely cared for. It has been an honor to give whatever voice I can, to life with AS. And it is my hope that this book, which serves as a sort of part two to *Pretending*, will bring the dialogue even farther, at least for females.

~

This book was not easy for me to write. I struggled with the content, the words and the metaphors I often use to illustrate my point. It was hard to talk about things I would rather forget. Calling attention to the multitude of ways AS has made my life problematic does make me sad, and it makes me worry I will say something that will make it seem I am hardened or irrevocably hurt by AS, when neither is the truth. I knew when I was writing *Pretending* that I had more to say, but the timing was not right for the kinds of disclosure you will read in this book. I chose to wait to discuss my big scary stuff, when I felt confident my daughters were old enough to learn what their mom went through. I also had to wait until my father passed away. For all of my 50 years, he was my personal translator and mentor. If he had learned of the things I talk about in this book, he would have been distraught and hurt. I could not have that.

I am more than halfway through my life. Perhaps that is why I feel ready and able and more determined than ever to talk about how Aspie women are wired, how we can be manipulated, how we can be chewed up and spit out, how we have to fight for our rights, and yet through it all, how we can eventually find ways to answer the call—who am I and what will I do to be who I want to be?

I hope I answer that call in a healthy way throughout this book. In each chapter I express my twists and turns with safety, covering as many issues as I could relate to from personal physical safety to maintaining a safe self-esteem. In the supports section I offer thoughts and tips on how to manage the issues that can too often lay us low, over and out. I also added a recommended resource section for those sources well worth a read.

There is nothing easy about having Asperger syndrome. It makes life in a neurotypical world difficult. It is frustrating. It is exhausting. And at times I want to give up and quit trying to make my way in a world that can be so cruel to people who are different. But those times do not last long. As a more than likely Aspie himself, Vincent van Gogh said what's in my heart when he wrote: *If you hear a voice within you say, "You cannot paint," then by all means paint and that voice will be silenced.*

This book is my painting. I hope it silences trepidations and moves away the things that go bump in the night.

Chapter 1
Healthy Relationships, Safe Socializing

Staying Safe and Well

What a sad part
A false friend plays
When she has to face herself
At the end of the day

—Barbara Nix

In *Pretending to be Normal*, I outlined my view of friendship. In a nutshell, I categorize friendships like I categorize my clothing. Some friendships are cozy soft sweater and comfy pants, let's dip our cookies in tea and talk about our favorite things, casual friendships. Some are dress slacks and a tucked-in shirt, meet me at a restaurant for steak and potatoes to discuss how we can help one another problem-solve a situation or effect a change friendships. Still others are high heels and long skirts and fancy baubles let's clink our champagne-filled crystal glasses when the clock strikes midnight, pretend to be someone else friendships. Easy enough to categorize in theory, but not so easy to do when it comes to real life.

Relationships have many different levels and sides. In effect, I see friends through pragmatic lenses. I realize neurotypicals (NTs) work from the inside out, that is from the heart to the head, but for me a healthy and safe relationship comes only after I have studied the person I want to connect with in a systematic way. I have tried the heart first approach and I cannot say those relationships have been my finest. I have to say they may have been my most intense and oddly exciting relationships, but in the long run they were the most explosive and damaging. Because

I think differently from NTs, I have learned it is important I build most of my relationships with people who either understand me for who I am, or with people who view the world similarly to the way I do.

I used to get dismayed when the cookies-and-tea friends would ask me to a fancy party, thinking they should know I am not comfortable at a big soiree. It used to bother me when someone I only really wanted to see once or twice a year for the ritual 'how is your family' kinds of questions started calling me for let's do lunch dates. Years have passed since I wrote *Pretending* and these days I have learned to bend my friendship rules—a little bit! I can't say it has become easy for me to keep my friendships footloose and fancy free, but I've gotten better at letting them take whatever form they seem destined to take. What I have not gotten better at is predicting which friendships, or any relationship for that matter, are destined for a breakdown.

~

One friend at a time was my adage throughout my early and teen years. It is so much easier to problem-solve a single friendship, than it is trying to juggle a lot of relationships simultaneously. On occasion I would get together with a group of kids, but it was a whole lot easier to focus on one friend at a time. Socializing in large groups reminds me too much of ants at a family picnic, only in my picture the ants are terribly disorganized and randomly clunking into each other. Too many ants are too complicated! When I am with one person, I can focus easier and relax more. More time spent with an individual gives me more time to figure out their views on the regular relationship-sharing issues like core beliefs, aspirations, fears and worries, and their goals and misgivings. Once I have that information, it is so much easier to think of things to say, things that will unite our relationship and keep it solid. Or, if after hearing their views on those important issues, I realize we really aren't of like mind, then I can tone down the relationship and keep our connection minimal and on a genuinely befitting level. The goal for me is to put effort into relationships that have shared interests and similar mindsets. I find all sorts of people interesting and worth more than a casual conversation, but my close relationships, the kind I give a great deal of myself to, they have to be set on stronger foundations. If not, I will for sure find myself embroiled in a combination of embarrassment, frustration and, eventually, bitter loneliness.

I suppose there are worlds where "once a friend always a friend" is a tried and true adage, but I have not lived in one of those worlds. My father used to tell me I was too naive and that my friends were really people who wanted to play with my toys or borrow my stuff. His history taught him early on that people were never to be completely trusted. He knew I was wired like him, and it was natural for him to worry about the way others would treat me. He had no intention of letting any child, or later any adult, grind their heels into my skin leaving nothing for me to feel but the pock marks their ugly intentions left behind. I spent many a year thinking Dad was overly worried about my relationships. I thought he was simply an over-protective father unable to realize his daughter could get along without his guidance. Turns out, Dad had learned to read people better than I had.

Soon after we finished our terminal degrees, my husband and I moved to a small midwestern town not far from where I grew up. My support system from my growing-up years might not have been living down the street from me anymore, but I felt a certain peace knowing they were only a few hours away. Generalizing, as Aspies do, I assumed this area would be very similar to the area that had kept me safe when I was a young one. At first blush, this new town was far too small and lackluster for my taste, but before long I was able to convince myself it did have a certain charm I could scoop in. The geography was virtually identical to the topography of my home town. The language had the same idioms and the community shared similar points of reference. The stores and restaurants were familiar, the popular sports teams were the same teams I had followed growing up, and, as an added bonus, a university anchored the town, which was exactly the kind of environment I found the easiest to understand. From all appearances, my little family was rooting in a very comfy and cozy spot. The first few years in small town middle of nowhere America, were spent pleasantly enough. Work kept us busy, life with a toddler and plenty of visits from my family kept us happy. Much like my luck growing up, I found my way into social circles thanks to the guy by my side. Just like with my boyhood friend Craig, husband Tom was a popular sort who had a widespread appeal. Men asked him to golf, women liked to flirt with him, and the town's movers and shakers considered him a peer. Tom had it made, and my pride never stopped me from riding on his coattails. Mind you, this period in my life was several years before I had even heard the term Asperger syndrome. Sure, I knew I had something distinctive and usually off-putting in my personality, but

I wasn't sure what it was. My mom summed it up best when she would say, *Liane, there is something about your personality that just pisses people off.* I knew most folks who were around me for very long would eventually look at me like I was a dizzy clown left behind by a runaway circus, but I kept thinking if I tried hard enough and observed people long enough, I could become part of the community without the help of my husband. While I took his help whenever I could, like so many women and so many Aspies before me, I truly wanted to stand on my own two feet and be accepted for me—the one and only me.

I tried so hard and at first I was able to tell myself I was doing OK as just me and not just Tom's wife. I was part of a ladies' clique and my daughter was invited to playgroups that moms seemed to want their kids to attend. My students liked my classes and gave me stellar reviews as a teacher. I can't say my fellow faculty accepted me as well as my students did, but I did have a few buddies on staff who made my days pleasant enough. I smiled a lot and practiced talking academia and current events until I could make a decent go of both in the real world. I thought I had figured things out, but of course I was wrong. Eventually the small town rumor mill let the gossip flow to my ears, and sure enough I started to see there was an ever so little but still powerfully painful difference in the way women behaved when they were around other women and when they were around me. I managed to find two real friends I will forever be grateful to for their kindness, but even they couldn't keep me comfortable in my own skin. The muscle of the majority was just too strong.

Once I knew I was the subject of rude innuendo, I quit playing my part as the innocent new girl eager to have a friend. I pulled back and tried to figure out who my genuine friends were. One of my two good friends took me aside and told me in confidence who I should probably steer clear from and who I could expect real kindness from.

My mother, the lady who takes no prisoners should someone decide they want to play too many mean girl games with me, came in and took over as my social coach. She made it clear to me the notion of mean girls goes beyond the teenage years and plays out well into females of all ages and in all places. Mom and my good friend saw who was being two-faced toward me and I listened to all their advice, except for when it came to one lady. Let's call her Brenda. I refused to believe Brenda was what my trustees said she was up until the day she finally wiped her feet on my sense of self…

I was crazy about Brenda. I mean, I really, truly and completely enjoyed being around her and worse yet, I was convinced she was a super good friend. She was so funny and stylish and cute and popular. We took off for girls' weekends, we shared lots of family-filled moments together, and we would spend hours talking on the phone like teenage girls do. It was so cool, in my mind, to have a fun friend like Brenda. It made me feel so special to know this lady who had so much going for her sought me out as a friend. Her friendship was enough to make me forget how unfriendly so many of the other ladies were to me. Brenda was that good! So I thought. Brenda, you see, could convince anyone she was with that she was exactly who they wanted her to be. A coy one, she was! And I bought her act, hook, line and sinker.

One weekend Brenda and her husband and another couple were invited to a weekend retreat with my husband and me. I would not normally do anything like this, but my confidence in Brenda as a friend was so high, I couldn't wait to push my luck and go one step closer toward seeing if I could finally handle a big social outing. My true friend warned me this was a bad idea, but I absolutely ignored her and decided I was up for the challenge. How could I fail with Brenda by my side? The minute we all met at the retreat, my heart started to beat faster than it should. All my instincts started to whisper I had better get the heck out of this situation and fast, but all my experiences with Brenda told me I was over-reacting. Ignoring my instincts, I stayed the course while Brenda tore me down. Brenda was no longer my friend when we weren't alone. She made fun of the way I dressed. She made fun of my not understanding what was going on in the big social chit-chat. She made fun of me until she ignored me. I'm not sure which was worse. I tried to shake the feeling of dread, but I couldn't. Not this time. I had given too much of myself and trusted Brenda too much. As hard as it was for me to swallow, I had to face the fact I had been played for a fool. Again.

I never would have guessed Brenda wasn't the lady I thought she was despite the warnings I had been given about her. Brenda's package was perfect for me and not just because she was the popular girl in our town. Brenda worked with special needs students that should have prepared her for a thinker like me. When my daughter and I were diagnosed with AS, I came to Brenda to tell her I needed her help with my daughter, and help for myself, but much to my shock, she told me we were not on the spectrum, and either looking for attention or making excuses for our problematic behaviors and issues. I cannot explain how badly this hurt me. Tony Attwood had diagnosed me by then and I was absolutely sure I had AS. The University of Kansas had diagnosed my daughter and I was absolutely sure she had AS. Why did Brenda believe otherwise? I will never know. It's been years since I last saw Brenda and I am still bruised by her betrayal. If Brenda had told people she didn't like me because I was odd, or if she had told people she was my friend only because she felt sorry for me, or even if she had explained she felt she had to act a certain way around me because she was afraid I was too fragile or volatile to take her any other way, I could possibly understand why the Brenda I saw was really just a holograph. Unfortunately for Brenda, *Pretending to be Normal* came out just as she showed her true colors to me. Our local reading group and the community at large read the book, excited to have one of their own selling books at the bookstores. Any questions anyone had about my behaviors, complicated communications or odd sensory needs were soon explained in black and white. Lots of *Ah, now Liane makes sense!* thoughts were let loose. People I thought never liked me came up to me and apologized for misjudging me. People I didn't even realize knew me started asking me for ideas that might help their unusual child, relative, friend or co-worker. In this case, disclosure set me free and bit Brenda flat in the butt. I'm sure she is fine and dandy by now, not spending one moment on thoughts about me, but there is a part of me that hopes she feels some remorse for betraying my trust and betraying my friendship.

～

The lessons I learned from Brenda and the small town we shared were not lost on me. Shortly after my daughter and I were diagnosed, my family moved to a new town in a new state far away; and when we did, I became a new person more ready and better able to define and recognize what a good relationship was all about. I know now relationships should make you feel many things, but never anything that attacks your self-esteem or your core worth. Keeping in mind that every relationship, no matter its origin or destination, length or depth, will have ups and downs—I have learned there are some general givens when it comes to relationship wellbeing.

Relationships should make you feel happy, secure and appreciated. When you are with someone you hope to connect with, you need to feel as though you are a better you, ready and able to face most of your days with a smile and optimism. Just as you give in a relationship, you should be comfortable taking, believing a relationship is a two-way street or a circle with lots of intersections, shared joys and goals, and the occasional forks in the road where you go your way and the other person goes a different way, but never in ways that destroy the path back to one another. Compromise should come even when it stinks to have to make a few concessions. Compromise should never come if that means you give away something that causes you pain or anger, or upsets your trust or confidence. Relationships are at their best when they encourage those involved to learn something new, just as they respect everyone's rights and privileges. They should give you the chance to openly share what you know, not just about yourself and AS and your favorite obsessions, but also about life and hopes and dreams and failures and tears and everything and anything of interest to you. Perhaps most importantly, relationships for Aspie women in particular, need to be honest, kind and supportive.

There might be very little that is easy about building a relationship, but if this is what you want, it is worth the effort to work toward doing so. If a strong personal connection to another person is not what you are after, that's OK too. Many of us enjoy our own company and are happy with the relationships we were born into and the relationships we have with our animals and personal interests and hobbies. But if you hope to have a job and at least play nicely with those NTs around you who may never truly understand or even accept ASD, you will need to know how to speak the NT social language.

Much ado is made over socializing, both when in a relationship and within our daily responsibilities at work, around the neighborhood, in travel and just about everywhere else we go. I have never been to a conference where I have not been asked how to help someone on the spectrum learn to socialize better. I readily admit socializing is an innate behavior for neurotypicals, but I also believe Aspies can learn enough social skills to get them through the demands of their day-to-day life. In fact, I think Aspie women can learn as many social skills as we wish, so long as we are willing to employ our innate echolalia skills and spend time learning about the social customs, expectations and behaviors that fit our surroundings. Please note I'm not making a judgment call here. I'm not saying we *have* to change who we are if we don't want to. I'm simply saying it can be very beneficial to our lifestyle if we learn to be socially bilingual. Aspie and NT. Able to turn on and off whatever skill sets we need when we need them.

If it does interest you to become socially bilingual, the world wide web will come in very handy. It is easy enough to access all kinds of information on virtually any event located in any area you might have to visit. Things like protocol, manners, customs and more, are shared on individuals' websites, group sites, local and regional community sites and among social science journals and magazines online.

We might not be able to feel calm and natural beneath the surface, but most women with AS can appear assimilated once we have memorized what others in the society we share will expect from us. I admit I sometimes feel like I am losing pieces of myself when I put the real me on a shelf so the side of me that society accepts more easily can get a job or make a not too terribly stressing appearance at a meeting or party. But I take pride in knowing I can be both Aspie true and NT on occasion. It is kind of cool to realize I can adapt and follow social rules, especially when I remind myself that in essence, I am showing a talent for being bilingual or bicultural.

I still make countless socializing mistakes according to the NT platform. But I don't focus on my mishaps like I used to. I picture Aspie women as they try to get along well with girls at a gathering, or with co-workers at a meeting, or with teachers and other parents at a school function, like I picture cold water splashed on a grill. On some days the grill is nice and cool to the touch and all is well and we are happy and easy go lucky. On other days, we find the grill is red hot, leaving us zapped away into little droplets evaporating before we have time to catch a breath. We know we have a right or indeed, an obligation to be in the fire as it were, but we can't find a way to stick to the grill and get the job done without being scorched away.

Socializing will never come naturally for Aspies and it may never be fabulously fun. However, socializing at a level that lets us get and keep our jobs, make general community connections, and network to a safe and useful point, can be achieved. The trick is to learn the secrets of socializing and to be OK with the reality that things don't have to be second nature in order for us to enjoy them and benefit from them. I can learn to socialize. After that, it is up to me to decide when to play the NT game and when to be all Aspie me. And so it is for you!

"Safe and healthy socializing" supports

Socializing is tough, tough, tough. Never mind the anxiety and sensory dysfunction that bubbles up when we have to gather in groups, the biggest issue for me is figuring out how to present myself in a way that won't leave me embarrassed. I've been observing and experimenting in the social world for decades now, and while I am not nearly a pro at the game, I can usually eke out an hour or two of decent time spent having fun without too much exhaustion hanging on till the next day. Each time I go out and about I have to think about what kind of support I should rely on knowing some work better than others given any number of variables. Clearly it is up to you to decide if you want to work on your social game. I respect the decision to reject the notion completely, but if you do think social tips are worth a look, here are some ideas I rely on that might help you too.

There are way too many social rules for me even to think about, much less write about in a book, but there are some things most cultures accept as practical social elements, some everyday common courtesies we would all benefit from. Even when NTs are guilty of ignoring these rules (which they often are!), I try to abide by them simply because they show respect for other people and attention to detail, and as my dad used to say, good old-fashioned polite behavior should never go out of style.

Make a nice first impression

First impressions stay with people for a very long time if not forever. I figure if people like me when they first meet me, it will give me some time to be appreciated for who I am, eccentricities and differences celebrated and not shunned.

- *Be on time.* If you aren't, be sure you have a darn good reason for being late and, whenever possible, notify the person waiting for you that you are running behind schedule.

- *Don't try to be someone you aren't.* This doesn't mean you have to make a formal disclosure to every person you are with. It just means it's cool to be you and, by being you, chances are better you will relax and have more fun—two things that will put other people at ease and make them have more fun, as well.

- *Don't be messy.* I'm not a big fashionista, but clean clothes and a clean body can go a long way toward making others feel at ease around you and I can't personally imagine wanting to be anywhere other than at home taking a shower if I smell myself stinking up a room!

- *Dress to code.* That is, if you are going to a formal event, check the dress code and don't be afraid to do so. I know people who ask their family to show up for Thanksgiving dinner in a suit coat or dress. That's not my cup of tea, but if I wanted to accept an invitation from the people who set that rule, I would be respectful and wear a dress.

- *Smile.* A smile is the universal sign for good things. Sure people can use a smile to hide sarcasm, predatory behavior, and a whole lot of secrets, but for the most part a simple smile is a welcome gesture few can find fault with.

Small talk

Try not to hate it. I try to learn how to use it to my advantage.

I found out a long time ago, probably after reading a self-help book back in the 70s, that people like to talk about themselves. Since I find people interesting things to observe and study, it is fun for me to play into those likes and ask others all kinds of questions. I am pretty sure I have worn out some folks with all my questions, but on the whole, asking other people things about who they are and what they like, is a whole lot easier and safer than trying to engage in a balanced give and take of information. This isn't to say I don't ever share my thoughts and obsessive interests; I do, but for small talk with people I am leery of or people I don't know well, or people who I don't think would understand the interesting facets of the AS mind, I stick with the who/what/where/why/how concerning their life. Three good things happen when I do this. One, I don't have to disclose much about myself in the process. Two, I can build a schema or personality profile about the person and from that, direct my conversation to interests we might share or to topics I have a healthy hunch they will be happy discussing. Three, this kind of dialogue keeps me in the position of power. It means I am directing the conversation and keeping discourse in areas I'm comfortable discussing or interested in maintaining. As long as I feel I can predict and then direct where a conversation is going, my nerves stay calmer and my anxiety stays low enough for me to have a decent time with other people.

TOPICS TO AVOID

I'm not sure why, but apparently NTs are prone to think the following topics are not meant for casual discussion:

- political viewpoints
- personal fears and insecurities
- past interpersonal relationships
- religion
- personal finances.

Some even believe these topics should never be raised at functions of any kind. Too bad for me, because some of my most favorite obsessive interests are in the list, but I'm learning (after decades of offending people without meaning to) that I should avoid these topics unless someone brings them up and seems wholeheartedly interested in an open debate. But even then, I've made some past faux pas by not knowing when to end the debate and close the discussion. It's clearly up to you to discuss whatever you like, but be warned these subjects stir up something in NT people I can't figure out.

TOPICS TO ENJOY

The topics below seem to flow nicely for everyone. They are sweet and simple and only occasionally make flare-ups pop:

- current events and trends
- TV and movies
- sports
- the weather
- books
- entertainment, like music and theater
- careers
- academic interests, like astronomy, science, history, art, zoology, etc.

Experiment with these topics and I bet you can find a way for your favorite interest to come up. Just be sure not to hog the conversation with things that only you want to talk about. I know it's tempting, but imagine how you would feel if someone only wanted to talk about *their* favorite interest and it bored the heck out of you. Eek!

Kind words

As simple as it sounds, say these simple words when they are appropriate because, truthfully, they are worth their weight in gold ink: *Please, Thank you, Excuse me, May I*. I like polite phrases like these and the sentiments behind them. They flow gently and open up a curtain to a time when courtesies were offered as a matter of course, not because we are fake or trying to be someone we aren't. These kinds of expressions and their intent say *You are worth my conscious effort to be polite and thoughtful*. I have found that when I use them, I can turn a shaky moment or a questionable time into a calmer situation almost immediately. To me, these old-time expressions are like a warm pair of mittens on a cold windy day or a cool fan on a hot day. They neutralize and invite good things.

Chapter 2
Falling Prey
But Not Falling Forever

We live during a time when technology renders us vulnerable to a new-age bully. Our computers and cell phones lend to these modern-day trolls a stomping ground more vast than the schoolyards or neighborhoods of our youth. Within seconds, the 21st-century bully is armed for battle. Though the avenues for the bully have widened with the advancement of communication devices, it is still the time-tested advice from Spectrumites that continue to guide us toward resolution when confronted with the bully's toxic behaviors. Sharing our personal experiences, challenges, encouragement and advice as it relates to this important topic will assist each of us toward forging ahead with greater resolve.

—Sharon daVanport

It took me decades before I could openly admit how many times others had victimized me. No one wants to admit they were a stupid sap. No one wants to admit they were taken advantage of. No one wants to look in the mirror and see the shadow of humiliation or heartache peering back. But when I finally allowed myself to see the multitudes of humiliating experiences for what they were, experiences put upon me without my permission or approval, I was finally able to shove them almost completely out of my mirror. Sure they still lurk around at odd times of the night or when I'm in a situation that seems too similar to a nightmare from long ago, but for the most part, I've learned to decide which memories get to hang on and which have to be put in an airtight box and placed on a shelf and locked.

When I do open a bad memory, I try like crazy to apply some cognitive restructuring so I can change my immediate reaction to how

I feel about the episode. My idea of cognitive restructuring is simple. I practice lots of reassuring self-talk and I substitute and/or add in a healthier new way of looking at the event. In other words, I find a silver lining (even if it's just a tiny little bit of silver) in the cloud. For example, when I'm having a strong day, I can look back at the night one of my close friends encouraged me to drink a few bottles of wine so he could get me into his car for the kind of trashy "fun" only an evil man could hope for, and convince myself the only real damage I suffered from that night was a sense of shock and betrayal. I go down a list of what could have happened and did not, and then I consider myself not lucky, but yet fortunate to have escaped perhaps being beat up or left on the side of the road after the "fun" was over. So too can I recall the night a deputy sheriff refused to accept no means no, without wanting to hunt the guy down and have him arrested for something that happened 30 years ago. The strong me restructures what happened so that I refuse any personal responsibility for what the deputy did. And finding the silver in this cloud, I take solace in the fact the man did not give me a disease or broken bone.

Sometimes cognitive restructuring is not as effective as I need it to be… During my third year in college, I took a bowling course knowing it would be a fun class and an easy A for my transcript. After class one day, my kindly elderly professor asked if I would like to see how the bowling machines collect and re-track the bowling pins and bowling balls. In solid Aspie form, I didn't think twice about turning down a chance to take such a cool look at machinery in action. Imagine my shock when the tour I had expected quickly turned into my professor giving me a tour of his nasty tongue going down my throat. Cognitive restructuring is hard to design in this story. It is a tough one to collapse and rebuild because it is exceptionally creepy and violating. Even though the professor's act wasn't terribly physical, it hurts me more because it was so mentally cruel. I have spent years trying to find my way out of this bad memory, years talking to counselors about it, years trying to re-think it into something neutral. While I do not advocate medication for stress, depression or trauma, I do take anti-depressants and anti-anxiety medication. For me, the combination of medications and many, many years of grieving, plus the bits of cognitive restructuring I can muster up for mental pain, brought me to a place where I can remember the professor's act without wanting to throw up.

No matter how successful I am at working through nasty events, in the end, I do realize I was tricked and abused, and indeed, treated like prey. And if for no other reason, this is why I try very hard to advocate for ASD awareness and educate people on the spectrum, especially the classically vulnerable Aspie females. The stories of abuse other females with ASD share with me are insanely numerous. I am wise enough to know abuse stories are not unique to women on the spectrum, but I worry most about my Aspie friends because we are made up of all the things that make it so hard to know when we are being taken advantage of, until it's too late. On some level, we are just the sort of human that sits like a wide-eyed doe too innocent to run away from the hunter. We tend to be the nurturers and the more passive of the sexes. Perhaps that is why we are so easy to abuse.

I tell my abuse memories to my audiences most of the time. You would think I'd be used to them by now. But it is still a struggle to get through the telling without almost disappearing into a kind of dark whisper where no one but me lives. I call it my physical mute. In this state I can still talk and appear to be part of the surroundings. In physical mute, my body is in robot mode and my soul sneaks behind a safe place until I can re-integrate into the here and now without falling to pieces.

~

We learn our lessons so slowly. As a group, people with ASD are not wired to generalize. Experiences do not transfer from one situation to another. For example, after my episode with the deputy sheriff, all I learned was that deputy sheriffs were not to be trusted. First of all, this lesson is far too specific. Who is not as important as how and why, but I missed that concept for years. What's more, my conclusion that all deputy sheriffs are bad people has to be false, (however, I will be darned if I can look a deputy sheriff in the eye without feeling creeped out). Frustration barely scratches the surface of how annoying it is to know I can go from one bad experience to another like the little silver ball slapping around a pinball machine. If only I could easily take what I learn from one thing, to a new thing. Generalizing is a very difficult skill to learn, but it is not the only thing keeping Aspies out of the quick-learn lane. We are mind-blind, too often desperate to have friends, unaware of mixed messages, and on some real level, forever handicapped when paired with the wicked neurotypicals of our world.

I have many life-gone-sour stories on my personal hard drive. The wide-eyed doe Liane is now a more than middle-aged bifocal-wearing deer, but she is still unable to spot a hunter...

Not too very long ago, I went into business with another woman. If you had asked me then, I would have told you it was a partnership made of everything right. We shared the same philosophies, had mutual respect and trust for one another, and perhaps most importantly, my partner truly seemed to understand my Aspie way of thinking. In fact, for the first time in my life, it felt like my AS was the whipped cream on the coffee—a special little morsel of yum that made the partnership even better. All the good parts of my AS were allowed to come out and shine, and that was the most awesome of treats for me. The business itself was a perfect match for me too. The product was a favorite of mine, the business plan was a natural fit and my husband and I were able to secure loans from banks that were turning other small companies down. Life, it seemed, was rolling down a long highway with nothing but green lights ahead. The first month was great. The second was OK. By the third month, things were getting fragile. I do not know how or why, but cracks formed and it seemed like every step I took made the cracks spread. The customers who I had come to believe were also my friends started sharing gossip about me, my ability to run the business, and my dedication to the company as a whole. The gossip about me hurt the most. The same people who used to call me quirky and endearing began calling me odd and nutty.

Within six months, the tide really turned and all but a few of the customers met in private with my business partner to discuss how to take the business from me despite the fact my husband and I held the loans. My husband, and even my young adult daughters, tell me they knew my partner and the customers were turning on me. They saw things I did not. They tell me it was clear the end was in sight. How did I miss this? Should I really have known? How do people you think are your friends sneak in and decide they want you out of their club? What did I do? Everyone knew I was the only partner taking a big financial hit every month because I was the only one contributing to the mortgage payments. I spoke kindly to everyone, I tried to laugh and enjoy their company, and still, something about me made them decide I was not of their ilk—no longer a member of their group. Instead of thanking me for keeping the business open despite the financial losses, instead of coming to me with their honest thoughts about my personality quirks, rather than working with me to befriend me and accept me for the kindness I believe I was offering—they choose to work me right on out of their clique.

I talked to my business partner, the lady I thought was my new friend for life, to ask her what I had done and how I could fix things. She told me the group thought I was weird. *You would be OK*, she said, *and everyone might learn to like you again, if only you would quit talking so much and asking so many strange questions.* I know I talk a lot, but I worked very hard to keep my conversations to the common interest we all shared through the business. I thought that was what I was supposed to do. It is, after all, the advice the social skills coaches suggest. I think I have a handle on what weird questions would likely entail, and I do not remember asking any questions beyond the basic who, what, how, where and why. I followed all the social skills I could imagine. My family who serve as my mentors, saw how I behaved and they, the most honest critics I have, insist my actions were still quirky, but not the least bit rude, ugly, nutty or strange. There had to be some other machine at work this time. The hunter, or hunters as it were, had found their prey.

It was my husband who told me it was only a matter of time before our clients would, as a group, take their business elsewhere. I thought he was the nutty one. I could not fathom the thought that my personality was strange enough to make almost two dozen clients leave en masse. My husband was right and I was wrong. On a Friday evening, the group got together with my then business partner and decided they were ready to leave. The next day, our business was empty. We did not even get a thank-you, a goodbye, or a better luck next time. Wow.

I found it so hard to see myself as a victim this time around. For weeks I went around shell-shocked feeling totally defeated and ostracized. I had felt those feelings before and it had taken me years to dust them off my skin. No, I told myself, I would not play the role of victim anymore. I took a long hard look at the relationships and situations intermeshed with my business associates. With my family's help, I was able to point to times I was held responsible for things I had not done. Digging a little deeper and talking to a few employees, it became apparent I had been used as the fall gal, or the person who all bad things were pinned on. Piecing together bits of stories from one source and another, the reality of the situation became clear: My business partner and her assistant had either consciously or unconsciously made sure they always came out the heroes and I always came out the poison every time the inevitable business conflicts came up. Ah ha! Once I knew I had been manipulated and undermined, I felt less injured. I continue to feel I was not given a fair deal or a real chance to make friends, but at least I know I did my best. I offered a good product at a fair price and that is more than a lot of businesses can say. My partner and her assistant saw a better opportunity elsewhere and they took it. Business, as they say, is business, no matter how mean it may end up. Absolutely, I am sure I did turn people off because I am too lousy at theory of mind and because I acted overzealous when trying to make my clients my friends. But I'm not going to beat myself up for that. They are not bad traits that make me a marginal person. I accept no shame for being a bit of an innocent, a bit naive. I am not wrong or bad because I am Aspie. I am who I am, and if others feel the need to go behind my back so they can ease into a better opportunity for their own pocket book, well the shame is on them.

~

My personal nightmares and my business affairs gone wrong are stories similar to many I've heard from other Aspie women. The players and themes may change, but the action typically plays out in similar ways with the Aspie at the undone end of the knot. The consequences of feeling like a frayed rope with no real ties to fair play can be life-long. The effects might not be obvious on the outside, but they will show up in some form. Ulcers, migraines, paranoia, phobias, neurosis and/or anxiety will form. The Aspie might lose the ability to trust ever again. And sadly, in far too many cases another chunk of Aspie soul will be hushed, damaged and left to wither. That is simply unacceptable. Like a duck shakes water off its back, we females on the spectrum, who are so often bullied and taken advantage of, must make a pact to shake all the junk and muck the hunters of this world would put on us.

"Bullied no more" supports

Bullying: (n) any physiological, verbal or physical abuse that involves one person or group of people unfairly and inhumanely asserting power over a weaker or unsuspecting person or "target" group.

Bullying is a true coward's game. Its roots go deep and its repercussions are wide. The stereotypical view of bullying involves schoolyard boys picking on innocent children for their lunch money or homework, but the problem is far more intense than that. As humanity ages and technology becomes more sophisticated, bullying has taken on new and varied forms that have the potential to go far beyond the schoolyard and into virtually every aspect of life. My father grew up with bullies with raised fists lying in wait for him and later had experiences with conspiring co-workers interested in making it up the corporate ladder ahead of him at all costs. I was a victim of mean girls, bad men and a few family members who found my naivety too easy to manipulate. I had people watching out for me throughout my life, but my protectors could not follow me everywhere, all the time. When they were there, I had smooth days. But when those who had my best interest at heart were gone, I ruffled. Just as I believe I made it to a place of happiness because of the support of family and friends, and I know I almost fell into a complete breakdown because of the bullies who made me their play thing.

Sometimes the bully is insidious and tricky, sometimes he is less subtle and much more obvious. No matter the form, bullying must be recognized, understood and ultimately stopped. It may never go away, but at the very least people on the spectrum should know the warning signs of bullying and the fastest way out of the entrapment. Bullying can involve any of the below:

- Verbal assaults, including name-calling; negative and unhelpful criticism about the way you look, sound or act; derogatory comments even if they are seemingly spoken in a kind way masked in sarcasm.

- Situations that force you or lead you toward being alone or isolated, out of the group, excluded from a shared project or event you were invited to, or ignored when you do find yourself in a group situation.

- Physical assault such as hitting, biting, pinching, kicking, spitting, shoving, tripping, punching, etc.

- Slander and libel talk. Creating gossip and innuendo based on lies that involves you or your reputation in a way that makes you look or feel stupid, bad, sad, ugly, misplaced or uncomfortable.

- Having money, personal items or intellectual property stolen or damaged by anyone.

- Being forced or coerced into a situation or behavior you resist or know is not the right thing to do. This is a very gray area that is difficult to recognize, but would include being talked into stealing something for a "friend," having sex with an associate, letting someone copy your work or being pushed into lying to protect someone else's mistakes.

- Experiencing any kind of communication or correspondence online, via the cell phone, in notes or in any anonymous or impersonal way, that is uncalled for or demeaning.

Try as we might, social interaction will always be a struggle for the Aspie female. We can learn how to socialize and possibly fly right under the "she's kind of odd" radar, but we will inevitably pay a price steeped in exhaustion and self-doubt. I like to have a fall-back position for the times I know I am going to merge into social mishaps or situations that are just too dang hard for me to figure out. And at the end of the day I remind myself it is OK for me to be far from perfect and perfectly fine for me to be who I am if who I am does not interfere with the rights and privileges of others. The following ideas keep me on a track I feel I can manage. Add your own ideas to the list and remember fitting in is very subjective. It's up to you to decide how you measure your social success.

- Set up a peer helper well in advance of your social gathering. I have a few friends who know my limitations when it comes to group activities and parties. I disclosed my needs early on in our relationships and I know without a doubt I can turn to these people for guidance when I need it. Usually this means they simply stand by me to help me figure out the side jokes and comments of the crowd, or they will keep me under their radar when we are at events, checking in with me to see if I'm doing OK, just like they would check in on the punch bowl to see if it needs refilling. Nothing too big and dramatic, just little things that make all the difference in the world! It's amazing how much my friends' casual concern about my anxiety level or my worries can help me make sure I'm in a place where fun and happy things can find me.

- If it isn't possible to have a peer helper to guide you, think about "paying" someone to go with you to an event you are nervous about attending. Payment could be in the form of money, or exchanging this favor they do for you for a favor you can do for them, or some other creative exchange of support. Mind you, this isn't to suggest you sign up for some sort of illicit or embarrassing escort service. It's about finding another person who is really able and ready to take time out of their schedule to help you with yours. A good option might be to ask an elderly neighbor or busy mom, who needs a break from her own home life, to go with you. You will need to disclose why you need their company at the event, but you shouldn't have to go into great detail. Just a simple reason, such as your being nervous going by yourself, or your not feeling comfortable going out alone, could be all you need to say unless, of course, you will want to rely on your companion to give you social tips. If that is the case, you will have to explain at least the parts of your AS that make socializing so difficult.

- Check into joining (or starting) a social skills group for women in your community. This could be a mixed-age group, a same-age group, a group sharing the same interests or any other combination that seems to fit. Try to get an NT to join you and moderate the meetings if you can. Otherwise, take turns presenting social skills lessons the individuals have learned or at least researched. At the very least, a social skills group can help you simply practice what it means to get along with others in situations outside of your comfort zone.

- Ask an NT friend to suggest movies and books that illustrate healthy socializing behaviors. Study the material and try to apply it to your own world, but try not to memorize and script back exactly what you've seen or read. My quoting TV lines as if they were my own was pretty quickly deciphered as a kind of odd thing to do. I still do this, but now I give credit to the movie or book so I don't look like I'm just a parrot of someone else's words.

- Join a community theater group so you can directly learn about things like eye contact, vocal delivery, facial expressions and other non-verbal maneuvers, taking turns in a conversation and personal space. You don't have to act in the theater company's productions.

You can learn about these things simply by watching the actors and listening to the director while you spend your time on some other aspect of the production like lighting, set design, printing the programs or anything else.

- Have a safe place and safe person you can turn to should a social event turn sour. Know where the police stations and fire departments are and get there quickly if you think someone creepy is following you from the gathering. Have an emergency contact on speed dial. Get yourself to a place where people know you and you feel safe if you are about to go into a meltdown or just need to unwind. And always remember, the moment you feel unsure about where you are or what you are doing is the moment you should take to put your peace of mind first and leave the event.

Pick your friends wisely

When a person is keenly desperate for friendships, it is not uncommon to misinterpret any kind of attention as the right kind. The intensity of our desire to have a friend or two can quickly put a fancy shine on the intentions of those who would hurt us—the bullies who make it their business to sink their teeth into our skin and yank us around until we are either numb to the offenses or literally a mess of breaks and bruises. Not so nice people, these bullies are. How sad and unfair it is they have the power to teach us we are unworthy of anything but the nastiness they heap.

REAL FRIENDS

Do not hang out with just anyone simply so you can say you have a friend. Along those same lines, do not be fooled by people who tell you they are your friend, but seem only to be interested in using your material possessions, borrowing money, or taking advantage of your talents in some way. Kids are famous for doing this to other kids, telling Aspies things like friends do each other's homework and friends do special favors like stealing alcohol or clothes for friends. There are all kinds of versions to this theme. Figure out if you're being used or if this is too difficult for you, ask an NT you trust. As for me, I have had to learn the hard way that no matter how much I think someone likes me, I might be dead wrong. My kids are my friendship barometers and they have never yet been unable to detect who is taking advantage of me and who really cares about me. If you don't have anyone to help you judge a person's feelings toward you, make a list of all the things you really want and need in a friend and make sure the other person does not violate one of them. No friends are better than friends who abuse.

DATING

In my perfect world, people on the spectrum would only date people they have been fixed up with by friends and family members. However, there are places and situations that are safer than others for making friends and building relationships. For example, family-oriented centers like the YMCA, when compared to going to a nightclub, a local rock climbing club, or a local bowling league tend to be safer places for meeting people who do not have ulterior motives in mind. That having been said, there are cruel people everywhere, so the person on the spectrum has to have a solid understanding of what constitutes good and inappropriate behavior and how to handle such behavior if it comes up. Remember that dating will often turn into something interpersonal, so don't underestimate the importance of sex education. Research and read up on sex and intimacy, sexually transmitted diseases, birth control, the urban myths surrounding all the above, and the importance of knowing "no means no."

Bullying signs

When I look at the above, it seems to me I should immediately know when I am being bullied, but that is not my truth. I wrote the list of bullying signs below to bring an objective measurement tool to the idea of bullying. By memorizing this list, I can more easily put bullying on a radar I can recognize. Go through the list and ask yourself: Does this apply to me?

PHYSICAL SIGNS

- torn clothing or backpacks
- ruined homework or employment projects
- bruises, cuts, bloody noses, bumps, black eyes, etc.
- gum, mud or other nasty things squished in your hair, clothing, personal property, etc.

- chunks of hair cut off

- name-calling on the internet, in person or behind your back

- scratches on your car or damage done to your personal property

- suggestions from others that you should do your make-up, hair-dos, and personal style in ways you don't see anyone else doing.

PHYSIOLOGICAL AND PSYCHOLOGICAL SIGNS
Are you:

- developing gastrointestinal problems, stomachaches, shaking, headaches, etc.

- showing personality changes

- creating frightening or violent drawings and art

- expressing a heightened interest in violence, weapons, violent films, etc.

- beginning to act like a bully

- showing signs of poor self-esteem

- exhibiting a feeling of disempowerment

- becoming insecure

- becoming more agitated and anxious than usual

- developing depression

- developing eating disorders?

A note for NTs
Because female Aspies all over the world are verbally and physically abused by their mates and people in authority without even recognizing the situation as abusive, other people in the community need to step up and help us out. Many people are vigilant anti-bully protectors and to them, we owe a great deal of thanks. Others turn their attention away from our plight, perhaps afraid they might get the bullies' wrath if they step in their path, or frightened their involvement will become something too big for them to handle, or only because they feel no nurturing need to stand up and do the right thing for another. This is when community programs that gather and cultivate a team of caregivers

educated to know how to recognize and deal with bullies, becomes so powerful. With numbers of others against him, a bully's power is diminished. Toward that goal companies, community administrators and schools should:

- hold mandatory bully awareness programs

- establish a zero-tolerance policy toward bullying (Note that anyone violating the policies should be fired, suspended or penalized in some other very serious manner.)

- create safe places where bullied individuals can go for sanctuary and confidential counseling and protection

- encourage the popular and/or influential leaders of the group to take on the responsibility of protecting those who would be, or are being, bullied

- provide safe alternative activities for the Aspie when supervision of individuals might be difficult (This could mean everything from providing special interest club meetings during open playground time in the schools to a quiet break room for individuals in an employment arena.)

- post video cameras around areas where bullying would be easy to hide or happen (Bullies are not nearly as brave as they would have one think, and the thought they might be easily caught can do much to curb their actions.)

- encourage strong self-esteem for everyone because bullies are often the people with the lowest self-esteem.

Never, ever assume any individual on the spectrum understands what a bully is or recognizes the signs she is being bullied. Beginning in preschool and continuing well into old age, Aspies should be directly taught to identify and block bullying behaviors of all sorts. In addition to all the supports above, influential people in the Aspie's life should:

- teach the Aspie exactly what bullying is and where it is likely to happen, such as in bathrooms, playgrounds and lunchrooms, at office parties, during after hours in work environments, at nightclubs

- ask the Aspie to show she understands what bullying is through a creative but explicit way, such as:

- a play, puppet show, song, or story
- an art project
- a program the Aspie herself designed to end bullying
- a personal narrative about a time she was bullied and how it felt
- a simple verbal vent between the Aspie and a friend.

- teach the Aspie to verbally disarm the verbally assaulting bully (A quick and simple comeback such as, *What did you mean when you said...?* or *Are you trying to be mean to me?* might move the bully off his/her game.)

- be certain the Aspie completely understands she needs to quickly report any acts of bullying to a safe peer, adult or co-worker who will take the report seriously (Explain this is *not* tattling telling and not something she can be reprimanded for herself.)

- encourage the Aspie to walk away from any situation that feels remotely unsafe or unkind

- role-play bullying scenes complete with positive conflict avoidance scenarios

- teach a code word to the Aspie she can give to a safe person if she is reluctant to make a more obvious scene out of the situation or afraid of what might happen if she is identified as the person who told on the bully.

Only when we see each other as equals willing to defend one another's rights and privileges will bullying end. Let's hope that day is on the horizon.

Chapter 3
Broken Bonds

For When Something or Someone You Love Is Lost Forever

Loss is never easy and oftentimes it seems without purpose that something we care so much for has been taken from us. But although we may be creatures of infinite capacity we cannot have everything all at once. Sometimes, things must leave and make way for other things, or people, to come along. These things too can enrich us, or better yet, show us our next place and purpose in life. Show me a person who has never suffered a loss and I will show you a soul that while happy and pure, has not bloomed into their fullest potential.

—Rudy Simone

True, kind, meaningful support is the buoy that keeps Aspies from floating out to sea. I clung to my parents during my early years to keep me safe from bullies, misunderstandings, misguided teachers and any and all things that might otherwise have roughed me up. As more of my AS came out, it became easier for my parents to see that my dad and I spoke a language my mom could not understand no matter how hard she tried. Dad, it turns out, was an Aspie like me. Taking our psychiatrist's advice, Mom put me under Dad's wing so he could show his little clone how to work through the neurotypical maze. Mom was the resilient buoy in our life, but it was my father who was my day-to-day translator, my teacher and the glue that held me together.

Dad always looked old to me, even when he wasn't. It was the wisdom behind his age that was old. Dad was an encyclopedia of knowledge who never let a new idea or trend go by without first cataloging it into his memory vault. Like a good Aspie, he knew he had to be a collector of knowledge if he was going to be able to make accurate hypotheses about life in general, and especially about people's behavior or intentions. It was amazing how much and how often the man studied. Every day was a day to learn something new, he used to tell me, and when I asked him why he didn't have many friends he would answer *There is no point in talking to people who can't teach me something new*. Of course there were people who could have taught him many things. He simply never figured out how to ask others for their knowledge. Dad's AS presented itself in obvious form. He loved his routine, literal mathematics and engineering and trains. He shared facts and information about his favorite subjects and interests. When people veered from sharing of facts to small talk, he assumed he couldn't possibly be interested in anything they might have to say.

Thankfully, I was his friend. It was me he took to the mandatory office picnics and me he took to visit his family on the farm near his boyhood home. It was Dad who ran my Girl Scout cookie marathon and Dad who talked to my teachers when I finished elementary school. At precisely 4:30 every weeknight we went to the same restaurant where he would order the same meal each time. Together we would follow spotlights and fireworks, fire trucks and sunsets. Dad taught me how to question everything and to assume nothing. On his 50th birthday, I started warning him it would break me in half if he died. Every year on his birthday and many days in between each one I would remind him to take care of himself because he was going to live until I could live without him and by my estimations, that meant he would have to live to at least 100. *Listen*, he would say. *You're going to have to face the facts. I can't live forever.*

He was right. And so was I. A month before my own 50th birthday, my father passed away. That was over a year ago and I remain as lost as a fox in a snare. I know I am trapped. I know I have to get free. Trouble is, I am not at all sure how to get loose of this empty feeling. I keep going over the things Dad taught me and every now and then I feel like he's still around sharing his wisdom and insight. It makes me sad and mad to know he is no longer here for me when I still need him so very badly. It is horrible waking up every morning knowing my translator is gone. Without him to guide me, I keep tripping on very shaky ground.

I wonder, was Dad as insecure about his position in life at 50 as I am at 51? Was he acting stronger than he was because he knew my eyes watched his every move just as my mind grappled with the lessons he never quit teaching me? Did my need to know, force him to learn? I think probably yes to all the above. Together we forced our way into the NT world, and when my daughter and later my cousin's daughter, joined us in this special Aspie club, we were stronger because we were larger in number and had more reason than ever to pursue, discover and achieve. In large part because of my dad, the three female Hollidays behind him are better able to carry on the tradition of turning Aspie life into NT-friendly living. Dad left a legacy for us to learn from and follow. He left us a path filled with potential. He also left a hole bigger than the moon in my heart when his death broke the bond between us.

It is no secret people bond tighter when they have shared a common struggle, a common thread of understanding. Refugees know this bond when they move together to a new country leaving all they know behind. Soldiers share this strong connection when they both know one without the other is only half as likely to survive. Victims of trauma can look at each other and without saying a thing, know there is a level on which they and no one else can sit and nod in mutual understanding. The bond my father and I had was a bit refugee, a bit soldier survival and a bit victim and it was also the great bond of parent and child. That's some strong bonding by anyone's imagination, but it is made even stronger because we were both Aspie. When an Aspie bonds with someone, be it another Aspie who lives a story like theirs, or with a caregiver who does all they can to understand the story, the bond is tangible. All sorts of good things can come from such a bond, but when it is gone, all hell breaks loose until too many of our pieces burn to dust.

~

Death is not the only event that can break a bond. People move, jobs change, friendships crash, and time can steal the opportunities we need to keep a bond strong. It's not the how we lost a bond that matters so much as the loss itself. Even if it was healthier on the whole for a bond to be broken (say a friendship grew too strong with a person who had a terrible influence on our better judgment) the result is still distressing at best. I was just a kid when I became drawn to a 16-year-old boy in my neighborhood. Boys of that age are way too cool and most always forbidden fruit for barely teenage girls, but I didn't care. I was completely taken by this young man and in no short order, I became obsessed with him. Not in a creepy way, mind you. I didn't hide behind bushes to spy on him or call him at weird hours of the night to see what he was dreaming about, but I did have a real curiosity about what made him tick. I had a keen interest in knowing everything about him—what he liked to do, what kind of food he liked best, what his favorite color was, what books and magazines he enjoyed, what his favorite hobbies were, all the normal things a teen with a crush wonders about. The difference between the normal teen crush and mine was that mine didn't end. Most crushes, I am told, are fleeting. Kids fall in love and fall out, as quick as commercials between television shows. I fell for years for this boy. I met other boys and I fell for them, too, but I couldn't get this boy out of my mind. Years after the crush started, he got married, had a child and joined the Marine Corp. I went off to college. But I never forgot him. Then one day, a few months after his divorce, he called to ask me out on a date. Everything in my life started to wrap itself around this boy, this man. After a bad divorce, he loved my attention, but not nearly as much as I craved every single thing about him. It's embarrassing to me now, but at the time, he was the only thing that mattered to me.

We dated for two years. I convinced myself I was all but married to the guy. If he had asked me to get on the back of his motorcycle and take off for parts of the world unknown with nothing but a sleeping bag and a jar of peanut butter, I'd have done it. I was hypnotized once and that feeling was very close to the way I felt when I was with this person. It was truly that skewed. Of course he broke up with me, no doubt smothered by my intense adoration and overwhelming need to be with him as often as possible. When he left me, I knew something in me had changed. I could feel my nerves start to unwind. I quit eating. Quit sleeping. Quit going to classes. Quit everything but breathing and sleeping, and frankly I didn't much care if I kept up with either of those chores either. Luckily, my counselor did care. At the end of one of my regular sessions, she told me she thought I might be suicidal. I still remember how incredible that thought sounded to me. Suicidal? I didn't have a gun. I had no pills, no desire to drive my car off a bridge. I wasn't crying and screaming all night and day. I was aware time passed with me not in it, but I didn't have a conscious wish to give up. I just quit conscious living. Twice a day for a month or so after that meeting, my counselor made me call in to report I was OK. I wouldn't have done as she asked if she hadn't told me she would have me expelled from school if I didn't. The only thing stronger than my inertia after the boyfriend left me was my need never to disappoint my father to whom school meant so very much. Thank God I felt that way. I may not be here if I hadn't.

I carried on with my daily calls and my counseling as if I was a chalk drawing on a busy wall. I felt like people were walking by me, rubbing their shoulders over my drawing or their backpacks across my likeness as, little by little, the chalk started to disappear until nothing but dustings remained. Dust. That's all I was.

Of course I was clinically depressed by this time. The broken bond between me and this guy made my world senseless, in which case all I could do was lapse back into myself where things were quiet and uncomplicated. I knew how to act with me and only me. I didn't know how to act as a girl without her crush, or a woman without the man she felt married to.

After much time, I did recover from the broken heart. But only because a better match for me entered my life. I replaced a long time love with a wonderful guy who remains in my life to this day. I believe the bond I had wasn't really about marriage or happily ever after, it was about the connection of needing to feel close to someone, really close. The kind of close that comes easy to NTs, but comes so fleeting, if at all, to Aspies.

~

Probably because of our perseverating nature, when we find a bond, we grow to it like ivy to a tree. It isn't an evil obsessive perseveration. It's more like a cherished luxury, a solid sense of honest-to-goodness wonder, to know there is someone out there with whom we can share our true selves in ways that are accepted and, if we are lucky, cherished. Too often we are told we are too challenging or difficult to be around. Perhaps this is what makes a good relationship turn into so much more than it should ever be?

Clearly, personal relationships are the most difficult to let go of, but I don't see any break in what I am attached to, as a good thing. I don't like change. Find me an Aspie who does! Right, it's not going to happen. Show me an Aspie who isn't rigid in their thinking. Not possible. There's little chance we are going to bend our thinking quickly to fit a new plan after our established plan is gone. My husband once asked me if everything had to be carved in stone, and I answered with a clear "yes." We bond to our ideas like we take to our interests and bond to our people. We glue ourselves to our plans and routines with the kind of sticky glue that no remover can dilute without making a big rip in how we see ourselves.

Dreams and goals gone bad can make for as devastating a loss as any human connection broken apart. All my growing-up years I talked about my dream to be an attorney. I didn't *think* it would happen, I *knew* it would. I watched all the lawyer shows on TV, read autobiographies of the famous lawyers, and took three years of high school Latin to prepare myself for the lawyer lingo. I entered student government, took debate classes—did all I could to get close to the way I knew attorneys went. Aspie logic is pretty well set up for life as a lawyer, so I'm very sure I could have made it, had it not been for that first year of college when my grades fell as low as my life did. Trying to get into law school after a solid year of sub-par grades proved to be impossible. Trying to get into law school after finishing a master's program with all As didn't change the reality that law school was not going to be in my future. A lifetime of dreaming and planning and wishing and believing was shot down. At my ten-year high school reunion everyone asked me where I was practicing law. Each time the well-meaning question was asked, a little ting hit my reality; my bond with my dream was gone forever. I went on to have a nice career as a professor and now as the owner of an equestrian center, but I will *never, ever* get over not being an attorney. I've had 30 years to accept the change in my long-ago plans, but it still bites like a beast.

~

When bonds are broken, taken away, left behind or forced from our hand for any reason, it is devastating. Each time one of my bonds breaks, I feel like yet another string holding me up from top to bottom is cut. Like a marionette, a part of me lies loose and slumped. Too many detachments and the chore of getting up and taking on another day becomes ever more complicated. Every broken bond breaks tips of trust off. Insecurities hang around waiting for these things to happen, for it is then when the plague of internal thoughts start to scream *You're no good! You're crazy! You can't be happy—you're just too weird!*

Life happens. It just does. Marriages end. Plans don't happen. Pets run away or die. Kids are kicked out of their clubs. Adults turn their backs on old friends. We all eventually experience a loss of closeness, the force of a change and the end of routines we are devoted to. There is no such thing as consistency in life, yet without a predictable something in our life, or a relationship with our favorite person or thing, life is a cheese grater. Maybe we can shoot for organized chaos, but that's about it. Particularly since losing my father, I have had to learn the hard way how to rebuild a form of contentment and happiness. I am far from being where I wish to be, but I am trying to remember the bond I had with Dad and all the wonderful things I felt when I had other bonds in place. The glow from those bonds is still alive in me somewhere, and when I tap into it, I can almost see a light at the end of the proverbial tunnel. And when I'm not crying over my loss or rocking with the pain and sorrow over so much being gone, I peek out and realize that each day I am one day closer to finding a new bond that will also bring me great joy. Maybe not the joy I had with my big bonds now gone, but joy, in whatever form it comes, is good and right.

"Easing the broken bonds" supports

Broken bonds leave an Aspie with fewer ways to feel attached. The loss of a parent, the loss of a love, even the loss of a job, or a dream, or an academic challenge, can leave us without direction. In addition to cognitive restructuring, here are some other ideas for dealing with a broken bond. Keep in mind when a bond breaks it is in some ways like a habit that has been instantly taken away. Since it takes approximately six weeks to replace one habit with another and six months or more to go through the grieving process, be patient with yourself as you give time a chance to form new patterns and connections.

Invest in new ways to stay connected

Change is scary and rarely good. Loss is unimaginable. Both will happen. Know this and know too that it is a waste of time and energy to try and undo the loss. Use your time wisely and create fulfilling new ways to continue with the essence of the bond you feel is forever lost.

- Start a scholarship in the name of the person or pet you lost or a scholarship that will help others achieve the dream you had to leave behind.

- Plant a tree in honor of your loss. Put a memorial plaque beneath the tree explaining what it is for so that others might stop and give their respect or be inspired to carry your broken bond to more places where it can be honored.

- Run, walk or bike a marathon that pledges to raise money for the illness or cause your loss is related to.

- Write letters of support, encouragement and thanks to the people who are living the dream you had hoped to live. My husband once stopped by the office of a professor who was studying things my husband didn't have the background to study. All hubby did was put a note of appreciation for the man's work on his door. It still makes him happy to know he affirmed the man's work with a simple note that said, *I respect your work and admire what you have done for the study of chaos theory.* I'd bet the note made the professor happy too. It's a win–win.

- Join or start your own group that works to end the way your loss happened. For example, Mothers Against Drunk Driving sprang up after the death of one woman's daughter to a drunk driver. There is powerful healing taking place when you turn your tears of outrage into the belief your pain can end the pain of others.

- Reach your goals through new avenues. I didn't make it to law school, but I made it to a place where I can still advocate and work to educate others about those things I would have talked about in a courtroom. Fine. I am not a lawyer. I remain committed to my causes.

Connect with your feelings

Try with all your might to connect with your feelings after a loss or let down. This will not be easy for many Aspies, but as females we are genetically wired to be in better touch with our feelings than are our males with ASD. We can do self-reflection and work on expressing our internal dialogue. William Shakespeare sent an important lesson through Malcom in Act IV, scene III of *Macbeth*: *Give sorrow words. The grief that does not speak whispers the o'er-fraught heart, and bids it break.*

TALK

Talk. You should not feel anything is wrong with you if you find it hard to talk to someone about your broken bonds, but realize that talking to someone you can trust is often cathartic. You cannot predict what the response will be, but hopefully it will be forthcoming and helpful.

- Try to find an outlet for talking about as much as you can, when you can. There are online groups for grief and loss you can try as well.

- Talk your thoughts into a tape recorder or MP3 player and give it to someone safe to listen to or hide the recording away in a shoebox. Think of your thoughts as having been moved from your heart to a shoebox in an attic somewhere.

- Attend a grief support group.

- Talk to a religious counselor, psychologist, mentor, life coach, etc.

- Make a visit to a nursing home or veterans' home if your loss was an elderly person.

- Join a book club or idea club that is focusing on the very bond you are missing.

WRITE

Think journaling and beyond. Write in the traditional way in a notebook; in the sand with a shell; in the air with your hand; with your fingers using sign language; in mud with a stick; on a table with string; on a mirror with shaving cream or lipstick; on a typewriter or computer; on napkins and scrap papers kept in a box or drawer. There is no right way to write your feelings. If one way of expressing yourself leaves you feeling untapped, try something else. I like to write poetry and little sayings. One of my grief sayings goes, *In your grief you will find a new way to reach your loved one and forever and ever his loving and teaching spirit will lift you up and sail you softly through your ocean of tears.* It brings me hope.

BE ARTISTIC

Build art projects in any way art works for you. I like collages made from different materials ranging from magazine cut-outs to bits of nature all mixed together and lying on a piece of cardboard in juxtapositions that tell a story, even if I'm the only one who can read the story.

Invent a game that takes you (and any players your game may need) through the ups and downs of dreams made real and broken, rebuilt and destroyed, changed and forgotten. There is a game called Life that hints at this message, but comes up short. Feel free to use a game such as Life for your model, just changing the game's rules and deck of cards to change the message and consequences so that it really fits your needs.

Turn off the clock

When my father died, I asked my physician how long it would be before I quit feeling like I could not go on. My doctor told me six months or so. The doc was sort of right. After six months my anxiety attacks did subside, but my grief kept humming deep and dark. It revs up at night to a full-on storm, but at least during the day I can keep others from knowing my despair. My best friend Maureen, having experienced her share of deep grief, taught me a very important lesson when I told her I was unsure of how long to expect the grief to grab me so darkly. She told me there is no limit, no right or wrong, no prescription for grief. I know Aspies like definitive answers and solutions, but in regard to broken bonds, there are none. All we can count on is one day at a time while we try our best to redirect our sorrow-filled emotions into productive ones that open new doors for our heart to enter.

Prepare for the trigger

I can watch an innocuous television show and see a peony on the set of the show and Bam!—tears stream down my eyes. Peonies have a special memory for me; a memory that is nevermore. Oddly, I can grow them and savor them in my garden, but when they sneak up on me, I am not prepared to deal with the engulfing emotions they will undam. All I can do is excuse myself when the unexpected trigger shows up, go to a quiet place, get a drink of water, take a restroom break, or sit and be patient until I can reconnect the dots that the trigger shot to pieces. When I'm back to the strong me, I can take the trigger and put it aside, knowing that it will come up again, and when it does, I will go back to square one and get my composure before I expect too much of myself. Some NTs can get used to traumas. They don't like it, but they can adjust their systems to breaks in their world. NTs grow up getting acclimatized to changes. As children they get used to their pets going, then a grandparent or great aunt, then a distant cousin, then a closer relative, then finally a parent. NT teens begin to discover how one job comes to a natural end or the economy bites the job's funding, so that by the time they are young adults and then career adults, they realize there is always a chance they will not be able to hold on to their favorite job without some upheaval. That's how it is supposed to go, and when death or a career or other break follows a natural course, many NTs can accept them as part of a cycle they are prepared to deal with. Some Aspies master the ability to predict, prepare and react according to a plan too. Most of us do not. Each lost job feels to me like the first job I lost. Every funeral feels fresh and brand new. One pet dying does not prepare me for the next pet to die. There is no getting used to trauma. Every new broken bond seems to sting as bad as the first, unless we give in to ultimate despondency and no hope. I'd rather face each break with great pain, then give in and give up to the point I only expect the bad to happen. There is no solid evidence Aspies can take one experience and generalize it to the next. Know that and give yourself a break when you feel like you are never going to learn how to accept the inevitable.

Prepare a kit of sorts that will help you through a broken bond. Scents, photos, touchy/feely items, a few poems and song lyrics, a tape of self-affirmation, a little book of daily prayers, a rock and a few personal items make up my comfort stash I simply keep in my bedside table drawer.

It's not about you

End any thought that tells you a broken bond has broken a sacred rule or that a break is a personal attack on your character or heart. Things happen. Life is not all about making individuals happy or sad. Luck passes some of us over. Happiness eludes many. It is what it is, and it can be anything time and events mix together to create. Of course you can affect your life, but the point is, do not let the course of living put potholes in your heart. Use your powers of visualization to "see" the pain and disappointment turn from something dark and aching to something pleasant. Visualize the pain as a hole, then fill it with soft sweet dirt, plant a beautiful herb or flower in the new dirt, water it with your tears and sweat, and watch it bloom beautiful.

Uncover the unknown that can drive you crazy

Aspies are notorious for wanting to have the answers to what, where, why or how. I like that about us most of the time. Practice has taught me these questions are not always appreciated or timely. When my young aunt lay in her coffin with some sort of mortician's wax piecing her crushed face together, I asked why her face was melting. I remember my mother screaming for my father to get me out of the funeral parlor, and I remember my father telling me the mortician's cosmetic artist had to rebuild my aunt's face with putty and other polymers because she had been crushed under her vehicle. I took the sentence in my stride, sad, of course, but also comforted with the explanation. Now, years later, I can see through my mom's perspective. Now I realize it is probably a better idea to investigate your curious side; the side that may seem insensitive to NTs but is really nothing more than your wanting to have answers to the stuff you don't understand. It comes down to waiting for the right time and the right place before delving into the thoughts and questions that might hurt another. For example, if you wonder what happens to a body after it is taken to the morgue, ask a mortician to take you through the process when you aren't at the funeral itself. Don't know what it is like to experience a firing? Ask a career coach or boss of a business to explain the system to you before you get a job, instead of asking a friend who was just fired. Wonder what happens when you don't get into the college you want or when you put a bid on a house? Ask an expert like a college counselor or realtor, not the person crying because their dream school or dream house was taken away from them. In other words, try to learn the rules of the game before you go to a place that deals with things the world deems extra sensitive.

Keep a leash on your loyalty

We are very loyal people and may find it hard to let go of someone who is forever gone, a boss who let us go or a desire we cannot reach. This loyalty might turn into a perseveration. The last thing we need when dealing with something we cannot have is a perseverating circle that revisits the situation over and over ad nauseam. Dealing with perseverations is difficult. If you cannot get beyond the circle of obsessive perseverating, seek professional help as soon as possible.

Sleep, please, sleep!

My mind counts over and over or sings a refrain of a song for hours when I am in the middle of not getting something I want or saying goodbye to something I miss. No matter how exhausted I get, sleep of the solid sort skips right by. I try aromatherapy or a warm bath and warm milk before bed. I avoid exercising hours before it is time to turn in and I try to keep all electronics off at least an hour before bedtime. But nothing on the planet makes me go to sleep when I am in a sleepless pattern. I know I cannot save up on sleep, storing it for later, though I do take advantage of afternoon naps and quiet time when I can get it. Some periods of no sleep are worse than others, and if I go without good sleep for more than two weeks, I will go to my doctor for a sleep aid. This is not a practice I enjoy and I do not advocate it, but it is my last resort I reach for when I am absolutely beyond exhausted. Without sleep, we cannot possibly find the energy to think straight and thus think beyond the obsessive worry and sadness over the loss.

Scream

Go to a place where no one can hear you and scream, cry, shout, toss rocks in a river, do something to exercise the frustration out of your system. This physical process can do much to release the physiological pressure our bodies hold on to when stressed and forlorn.

Release and goodbye

Send a note you wrote or memorial you built into a farewell fire. Native cultures have done this for eons and it is a great symbolic way to formally send out a representation of the breaks that are bugging us. This can be very liberating. It is a symbolic gesture that can have as many levels of meaning as you choose.

Release and send forward

Just as you can release something to symbolically forget about it, you can release something to spread the inspiration from it. For this idea, learn an origami shape, but before you make your folds write something inspirational, healing or philosophical about the broken bond. Writing prompts can be inspired by poetry, photos, cartoons, memories, a religious book, songs—just about anywhere and anything can get you started.

When you have finished your prose and shaped the paper into origami, set them out on park benches, in mass transit seats, at spas and saunas, in public restrooms, in a big bowl on your counter, and anywhere else you can think of. You might make the word "Open" visible somewhere on the shape to encourage a reading. And hopefully, when others read the inspiration or lesson you are sharing, they will carry your dream forward to a place where at least someone can carry on the bond you lost.

Chapter 4
Mood Marauders

Or How to Ruin a Perfectly Good Day

Feeling incensed with loneliness in a socially brimming world
Never Alone, Never Connected
Drifting in Isolation
Only to find the common greeting of a mood disorder
Deceptively controlling our lives
And elusive to escape from its grasp
Yet owning our desperation can be the path to hope
And when so fortunate, contentment

—Rochelle Manor and Michael Wolff

A friend once asked me if I thought Asperger syndrome had an Achilles' heel. I had to think about it for a while, because there are several bits to AS that don't always play friendly. It is surely difficult trying to figure out non-verbal communications. Literal thinking is always a challenge. Most of us are never thrilled when we have to leave our favorite routine for too long. And it is certainly hard to memorize and apply social skills. But as far as the real ankle biters, I'd have to say mood disorders can become the most powerful cripplers for women on the spectrum. Clinical psychologist and autism expert Dr. Richard Howlin, agrees: *Given the ongoing sensory and interpersonal challenges, women with AS are more vulnerable to stress-related illnesses such as anxiety, depression and chronic fatigue syndrome* (personal interview, April 10, 2010).

Dr. Howlin knows his stuff! There is no doubt in the medical world that too much stress or even stress mishandled, can become the big black hole that will suck in your good health, balanced moods, work responsibilities, friendships, sense of self, confidence, and just about any other building block of happiness you can think of. I know this all too well. I suffer from a host of physical and mental stress-related ailments. I have long bouts with major fatigue. My immune system is precarious at best. I suffer from migraines that last 72 hours to the minute. My leaky gut, so common among people with autism, reacts very poorly when under stress. In fact, my gastrointestinal doctor tells me stress played a significant role behind the loss of my gallbladder and the removal of most of my sigmoid colon. Some days I think I am losing parts of my mind to stress too.

I've been in and out of cognitive behavior therapy for 40 years and while it has helped me deal with many issues, I have yet to find the key that will lock stress out of my life. When I am under too much stress I scream until my throat is raw. I walk in circles around and around until I get dizzy. I whimper like a scared puppy. And when it gets really, really bad, I take a sharp object like a key or my fingernails, and I dig into my forearms until welts show up. If that doesn't work, I bang my head against a wall. Fifteen years ago, stress led me to a nervous breakdown...

～

I don't clearly remember the circumstance that brought me down. I know it had something to do with my Aspie daughter's difficulties. Her little self had such tough times, such strong reactions to changes in routine and broken rules. Temper tantrums were her very common reactions to most anything and everything. She has her temper under control now and, thankfully, she doesn't remember her meltdowns; I don't want her to feel any guilt for the charged atmosphere of our home back then. But I remember them as if they just happened. Fear and tension and sadness and anger combine in a mom when one of her kids is so completely out of control. Words really cannot express the feeling. My memory can picture it, and often I relive the feeling, always worrying, always wondering—will they come back? Will her moments of disorientation and violence return? And if they do, will I be better able to handle her and help her? Or will I once again find myself sitting in a doctor's office trying to focus on the words coming out of his mouth, acting like I'm coherent, knowing I am lost in a fog thick and sticky.

～

My daughter's difficult time created a huge stressor, but it doesn't take a major ordeal to create overwhelming stress. Stress isn't usually caused by one thing, but rather by all sorts of things. Anxiety, the Aspie albatross, is a certain stressor. Anxiety quickly turns into nervousness, fear, worry and apprehensiveness. Situations that are much ado about nothing to NTs are nail biters to us. Neurotypicals make living look so easy. But it isn't! Everything gets so complicated and changes so fast and so furious. Cell phones, computer systems, trends, fashion, hairstyles, make-up options, threats to public safety, road detours, job expectations, medication needs, blah blah blah blah blah. When does it end?!? I'm getting anxious just writing this chapter, proving anxiety wreaks havoc all too easily. Extreme anxiety can make a productive member of the world into a person too nervous to face their co-workers. Anxiety can turn a healthy and productive Aspie into a housebound recluse who cannot step a toe outside of her bathroom. Too much anxiety can build and boil and eventually splash all over all things good in a life. Sounds extreme, but it happens all too often. Eventually, we begin anticipating an anxiety attack before we are even embarking on a simple journey.

Anxiety disorders are not as dark as depression is, at least not as far as I'm concerned. But they are more frightening. Depression for me is a scary calm, too much sleep and hours of endless mindlessness. Anxiety is speed in my system and panic attacks.

No matter how solitary our life is, the woman Aspie has some responsibilities that will demand she face the potential for anxiety head on. Sooner or later she will have to leave the shelter of her quiet space and go to her job, the children's school, the grocery store, the doctor's office or any other ordinary place. Sure, we can make up some reasonable excuse to get out of our responsibilities for a day or two, but eventually we have to buck up and get back on our life's course. We can't afford to stop practicing social communications or to stop living within our personal definition of constructive. If we do, we regress toward a more challenging and exhausting state of autism.

Some days I feel so empty, I picture myself curled up and creased. I get scratchy and uneasy inside and then I crash heavy. Even when I manage to paste on a fake smile, trying my best to not let my inner demons snare anyone else, my family can always tell when I'm not in great shape. But what can they do? How can they help? I haven't come to a precise answer for that conundrum, so we just settle for me climbing to the back of my closet for some dark empty time. At least that way I figure no one but me has to see the ache in my eyes. When the beast is roaring, there is nowhere for me to go but inside myself, mute, quiet, off.

Depression for many of us is a giant tidal wave just off the horizon. The smallest change in our course can stir it to shore. I have to be very careful with my mind or it will take me to places that encourage depression. When I flip through the visuals in my memory, I have to flip fast just in case I call up something that still reeks of failure, rejection or sadness. I won't go so far as to say I'm a martyr, but I am a human with feelings that are still scabbed from the times I was treated unfairly or rudely simply because I am a few deviations off the norm. It can be very hard for me not to feel sorry for myself. I'm not sure I could resist the temptation were it not for the fact that I fully realize I am far from being the only one on the planet feeling dismayed.

Like many females on the spectrum, I am very sensitive to the untouchable feelings of others. I can walk into a room of strangers and within moments, be drawn to the person in the most psychological pain. It feels like some weird sort of vortex is pulling their energy into mine. Maybe I am homing in on a look on their face that is below the obvious. Maybe I can just sense things at a sort of innate below-the-superficial level much like an animal does, but a neurotypical would not, or even cannot, fathom. I don't know how Aspie women do this, but I do know many of us can simply sense when someone is fighting his or her own deep troubles. And when I sense these things, I absorb their troubles like a sponge. It's a fatiguing ability I wish I didn't have. If I had the skill set to put a person's broken world back together, I would embrace all the icky that comes with this knack. Regrettably, all I can do is sympathize, listen, and offer some words of advice I've picked up from one of my counselors or friends. I understand that is typically all a person expects from another person—a good ear and some consoling, but for me the result is damaging. Even if the person in trouble feels better from having shared with me, even if they feel the unburdening has taken the pain away, I never feel cleansed or better. It's like my heart is a topiary and the sad stories are vines that grip my branches and grow and wind and twist their way into the other stories I've heard which lie on top of my own painful experiences until the whole topiary grows thorns and a thickness I can't cut through.

~

The extra sensitivity to others' moods strikes me often, but so do other influences that are equally damaging to a content peace of being. People with AS tend to have exceptional memories. Some say photographic memories are actually common to Aspies. I know the people on the spectrum who share my bloodline, share an uncanny ability to recall the most minute of details about the most mundane of things. While we may struggle with the main idea of a paragraph or the clear point of a line of reasoning, we are typically able to vividly describe just about anything we see. Ask us what happened ten years ago at a family reunion attended by 100 of our closest relatives and friends, and expect to hear descriptions about the bizarre print of Aunt Sally's smock, or what cousin Joe said while eating with a mouth full of potato salad, and how Great Grandma's stories sounded breathy and so sophisticated when whispered through her bold drags on her stinky cherry cigars. Memories stick in our brain like mud sticks to a pig. I suppose this is the product of a mind that settles not on the superficial, but on the things that draw our attention; the things most others take for granted or never even notice. For the most part, I like taking in all the details and nuances I can gather, but there are times I wish I could remove the part of my brain that masterminds this power, the part of the brain that thinks in pictures.

Temple Grandin told the world about thinking in pictures and in her brilliant articulacy she explained how her brain holds on to things she sees. On the surface, it sounds like this is a really great gift to have, but those of us who have it know it does not come without a cost. We cannot edit one frame of the saddest thing our mental library of scenes holds tight to. Some pictures, when viewed too intently, can weaken the strongest soul. A television commercial about an abused dog or the cover of a magazine showing pictures from an earthquake-torn country, or a photo of a child standing all alone in a corner on a busy playground, can send me down low, below-the-ground low. Depression comes on strong then and there. The fatigue sets in strong. The perseveration cycle in my Aspie brain replays the troubling scene(s) over and over and over again. It doesn't matter where, what or how the unpleasant image is brought to my attention, I am pulled to it and so my chain of sad, horrific events becomes longer and tighter and heavier.

People have asked me if I would get rid of the gift of a fantastic memory system if I could. I don't think I would. I cherish my collage of good memories. But there are times I wish I could make myself selectively blind, like I can make myself selectively mute. The depression that drips from sad images and sad memories has the power to make the good memories jump around and jiggle just out of reach, like a bad carnival trick where there is never a winner.

~

Just get over it. Don't think about it. All you're doing is causing yourself misery. That's the advice I hear over and over. It's solid advice and worthy advice, but depression is a tricky minx and my experience does not suggest there are any quick or easy things an Aspie gal can do to get rid of it.

Mood disorders in all their many colors and incarnations, must be taken very seriously. Firm research has not concluded how many women with Asperger syndrome have contemplated suicide, much less how many have succeeded in taking their lives, but I've heard experts in the field suggest up to 80 percent of the ASD population has talked about suicide at least once. I am among that 80 percent. If you are, too, put this book down and immediately contact a friend or suicide hotline for intervention. Do not be afraid or ashamed to do so. Obviously it is essential a qualified expert be consulted when any mood disorder begins to interfere with your quality of life in any way, shape or form. Remember, there is no shame in seeking help. I tell my three daughters all the time, if your ankle hurts, you would not think twice about going to the doctor to assess the damage and get a prescription for rehab, so it logically follows you should see a doctor if your mind hurts.

Mood disorders are nothing to be ashamed of. Almost everyone on the planet will face a challenging mood at sometime in her life. I know it is very hard and very frightening to admit to having a mood disorder, but if you don't, how will you ever get the help you need to end the pain? The fact is, when a mood disorder is up and running, the neurotransmitters serotonin, noradrenaline and dopamine get lost in the race. Let a qualified counselor, advisor or doctor help you get everything back on the right track. If you do, the chances are actually very good you will be able to control the disorders that plague you.

"Mood marauders" supports

One of the ironies surrounding mood disorders is the push and pull of the feelings they entice. Mood disorders tend to make a person uninterested in her daily activities, hobbies and healthy lifestyle. Ironic, because without engaging in these things, the moods will only get worse and hang on longer. It is incredibly difficult to push through a mood disorder to get to any semblance of a life once enjoyed. But if you don't try, you'll never get back to a healthy place. My father used to advise me to take one day at a time. To that I add take one step at a time, until you are taking the steps you need to be happy and healthy. Go step by step with the ideas I have here so mood disorders find it harder to settle in and disarm you.

Exercise

When I work out with weights, swim or clean up after my horses on a regular basis, I find I sleep better, smile more, think brighter and stress out less. There is good reason behind my mood elevations. The weight training makes me stronger and less fatigued when I go about my daily living, and I have to admit I just feel happier when I look in the mirror and see less paunch around my belly. The horse cleaning and swimming increase my cardiovascular health and this in turn increases my endorphins. Mind you, I don't go crazy pumping iron or completing marathons. Some people have to work out harder and some even less, in order to feel their mood lift, and as it is always important to check with a doctor before beginning any new exercise routine, I suggest women work with a physical fitness specialist to design their own individual routines that will work for them. Remember, what works for men, may not be the best bet for women. Our bodies and what we put them through are far different from the males' and it is essential we respect the limits we can push ourselves to, and essential we learn which exercises support our body types, hormone fluctuations and health history.

Giggle

Trust the studies showing laughter boosts the immune system and the release of endorphins. Watch favorite funny shows, learn how to tell (and understand!) jokes, read comics or play games that make you smile. If all else fails, fake a laugh for a few minutes and chances are good you might give yourself a case of the giggles.

Medications and food supplements

Keeping in mind I am not a physician, I try not to advocate for or against the use of medicine with regard to mood disorders. I make my decision on which medications to take, only after I've done exhaustive research on the subject and spoken at length with my physicians. However, I feel comfortable saying it is a smart idea to check your diet to be certain you are taking in the appropriate levels of vitamins (particularly the B vitamins), amino acids and minerals. A good one-a-day vitamin is my best friend, but I am always careful to tell healthcare workers I am taking vitamins because even the most common vitamins can interfere with the absorption of certain medications and also have an impact on surgery success and other health issues. The bottom line is—do not automatically put all your trust in the natural supplement and/or pharmaceutical companies. Educate yourself, talk with your doctors and learn to study your body to see how various medications make you feel, should you decide the time is right to add medication of any kind to your life.

If you do decide a pharmaceutical anti-depressant medication is for you, beware: they are not magic pills that work miracles overnight. Most of us who take medication have to experiment through several trials to find the best drug to fit our needs and virtually all of us have to wait at least a few weeks before we feel any noticeably significant changes in mood. And know too, that drugs alone are typically not nearly enough to make real lasting changes in depression. A combination of the methods described here, in addition to other treatments your care staff recommends, will pave your way for the healthiest recovery.

Environmental therapy

Create the environment that brings you harmony, good thoughts and peace of mind. Consider all your senses and build from there. I rely heavily on my sense of smell and my auditory needs. Complete quiet and lavender cucumber smells work well to de-stress me. I admit these measures, combined with a view of a vista either in my mind, in a photo or in real life, do wonders to calm me, but not if I am in an overload mode. I find environmental therapies are great as preventative measures and great after I am over the worst of my bad moods. I have female Aspie friends who rely heavily on their sensory environmental measures to feel better no matter where they are in their mood cycles. Experiment to see when and how you can use your senses for your benefit.

Breathing

Breathing sounds ridiculously simple, but many people with AS actually do forget to breathe until their lungs demand a gulp of air. When the body doesn't breathe it gets the message the body is in dangerous flux. This upsets the respiratory wellness we need to help rid the body of toxins, build energy, clear our mind and improve our mood. Practice the age-old, slow, deep daily breathing exercises taught in tai chi, yoga, prayer, qigong and meditation to help you use your breathing as a natural, free and liberating way toward better moods. Or give kapalbhati a go. Sit on the floor with your legs crossed, take five deep breaths in and out through your nose. When you have taken your last breath in, quickly exhale ten short bursts through your nose. As you breathe in think, *In with the good*, and when you exhale, *Out with the bad*.

Grounding

Yogis teach the practice of placing a heavy blanket across your chest as you lie down to rest and restore your energy and inner balance. Sensory integration therapists use the same principle. Try it for yourself and add a soft cover over your eyes if you enjoy the sensation of pitch blackness. Experiment with the weight of the blanket, but keep in mind it would be unsafe to put something beyond a few pounds on your chest.

Modified cognitive behavior therapy

When I face a situation I am struggling ever so hard to improve on (more than likely it is my inability to think before speaking my mind), I tend to get overly anxious over my weaknesses. Sometimes, I become selectively mute or reclusive just to avoid others seeing me without my NT mask. My father used to remind me that all the bad emotions in the world will do nothing but make my attempts to fix something that much harder. Dad used logic to set me straight. In particular, he taught me how to restructure my schema (the sense of one's experiences), how to modify my behavior to fit a situation, and how to problem-solve my way through life's challenges. In effect, Dad was using his own version of modified cognitive behavior therapy (CBT) to help me with anxiety and depression, and to teach me how to cope with, and fit in to, society and its demands. A solid discussion on CBT needs a whole book to be complete. I suggest a few in the Resources and Recommended Reading section of this book. Research the method on your own and in the meantime, work with the following principles to begin your growth toward happier mental health through CBT.

EMOTIONAL RE-DOS

Study your emotions in response to a variety of situations and decide if you made an appropriate response or one that might be misconstrued as inappropriate. Note, I said "misconstrued." Aspie women do not try to make their mark by offering insults or saying rude things, but too often that is how our comments are perceived. It's our honesty and our straightforwardness that accounts for much of these misunderstandings, but sometimes too much honesty is too much for too many. My mother tells me *The truth may set you free, but that doesn't mean it sets anyone else free.* She has a point. When I worry I may have offended someone, I go through the range of emotions my message was supposed to convey and I ask myself what other words and gestures I could have used to better convey my intent. Let's say a friend tells me she has to have minor surgery, and my response is to tell her about all my major surgeries. My intent would have been to reassure her, to let her know even major surgeries bring recovery sooner or later. But my friend may have thought I was trying to say she was being silly about worrying over something minor or that I was implying I was a tougher woman than her because I had been through more. I realize I have poor theory of mind, so I self-impose a flowchart of all the ways my words could have been understood. I try to remember, in communications there is a sender and receiver, but in between there is a whole lot of room for error. Once I know I've upset someone, I will talk to the person again, admit I may have said the wrong thing and then re-explain in different ways, what I really meant. Sounds complicated, but it really isn't. It's just like re-writing sentences in grammar school. It's merely finding more than one way to express an emotion. Easy peasy.

PICTURE THIS

Draw, sculpt, paint or create something tangible that helps you comprehend and internalize why you are feeling upset, anxious or angry, and then make something tangible that expresses how you can go about feeling better. I'm not an artist, so when I use visuals like this, I tend to cut out photos from magazines and write blocks of descriptive words around the photo to really sculpt what I'm thinking. If you think more symbolically, express yourself with whatever designs make sense to you. Just be sure to include the stumbling block or problem you are facing, the solution(s) you come up with, and the intended result. For me, that might mean a photo of a woman looking hectic and anxious, followed by photos of women exercising, eating healthily and grooming a horse, followed by a woman sleeping with a smile on her face. Eventually, I try to jump straight to a photo of me grooming my horse to make me feel better. The train of thought brought on by the photos becomes something akin to a muscle memory I can call on in short order when I need to.

JUST THE FACTS

Avoid assumptions. Let's say someone comes to you and tells you they heard a group of your mutual girlfriends were talking about you at a party. The friend tells you she could not hear what the girls were saying, that she only heard your name mentioned twice, but that she could tell by their body language that the conversation had to be negative. Rather than believe this right from the get-go, sit yourself down and ponder— what other possible explanations might there be for this scene. Write your hunches or hypotheses down on a piece of paper if it will help. Could the ladies have been angry at the way someone else was treating you and so they were actually coming to your defense against the rude party? Could it be the anger was aimed toward a different situation they all knew about, and they were mentioning your name as a way to include your positive energy and helpful abilities, implying *Jane needs to know this is going on. She will help end this drama.* Or could this situation have been completely misunderstood and there is someone else who shares your name, in which case you were not even the person the ladies were referring to?

My point is simple. Even if you personally hear and see a situation unfold, it is possible you misunderstood the intentions or innuendos of the interpersonal and group communications. Jury deliberation proves my point. If everyone understood what they heard and saw the same way, there would be no jury deliberations. The next time your mind tells you something is going on, really analyze the situation and see if your mind might not be playing tricks on you. But if you come to the conclusion you are dead right in your belief, ask someone you believe in for his or her opinion. Only after you have gotten a consensus of agreement, should you declare your thoughts are accurate and, at that point, convince yourself to see the situation as a challenge your intelligence, wit and logic can handle with productive results. Just be sure you don't stress out and grow overly anxious or depressed about the situation or perceived situation. Those feelings will not manifest any positive force or thinking that will help you fix your world.

ACCEPT THE SITUATION

Sometimes there are problems or obstacles we have to admit we struggle with. Once we admit we have an issue, we can then cultivate the tools we need to overcome the issue. Many females with AS say the diagnosis of Asperger syndrome gave them the green light to begin rebuilding their coping mechanisms, understanding of the world, and ability to interact successfully. The mere acceptance that we are different gives a certain sense of freedom; a new highlight in who we are so that we can become who we wish to be. Be honest with yourself when it comes to taking a personal inventory, and if you have a problem, don't beat yourself up over it. Instead, consult with others, do some personal assessments, put together a treatment plan, join a group for therapy or support and get yourself on the path to the life you wish for.

I often say about myself these days *My life is what it is*, and in that simple statement I find I have the luxury of accepting my faults and trying every day to learn something from my failures. I do not always succeed. Far from it. But I always try, and trying is a virtue I am proud of. As my dad used to say, *Did you do your best?* If the answer is yes, then be proud of yourself and the next time you have a problem facing you, try just a bit harder to work on it.

Yawning

When you yawn, your body releases the neurochemicals oxytocin and acetylcholine that can calm stress. Practice yawning 10 to 15 times in a row with a short pause in between each yawn, and you will reduce your stress to a level you will be better able to handle.

Guided imagery

Based on the Buddhist philosophy that has always taught the mind and body are connected in ways we can only begin to imagine, guided imagery asks the human to direct and guide their thoughts, using as many senses as they possibly can, to a place of harmony, optimism, health and relaxation. Lest you think this is a foreign concept too out there for you to really benefit from, think back to your early childhood when you might have lost track of your teacher's lesson, going instead to a story in your own psyche where perhaps you were the princess of your castle in the clouds where the land smelled like cherries and the carpet under your feet felt like cool mushy clay. Quit daydreaming, your teacher would have said. Return to your favorite place and resume guiding your images, the Buddhist would say.

Relax your body, empty your mind, and rebuild your emotions and thoughts one stage at a time. Set the stage for your images if you need, by looking at a photograph of a favorite memory, or listening to a beloved song, or even smelling or touching a favorite object. I like to look at a painting filled with rich color and movement before I begin my meditative guided imagery. With the painting in my mind, I form happier thoughts to replace my anxious or depressed thoughts. I picture my favorite things popping up in the fluidity of the painting's movements, perhaps a horse running in what I will see as field, and a fountain of chocolate so close and fragrant I can almost drink from it. With the happy images in my mind, I can feel my body start to relax and rejuvenate on the spot. Relaxed, newly energized, I can then attempt to learn something from the anxiety-provoking situation. I can try to think of ways to keep the situation from repeating itself. And perhaps most importantly, I can forgive myself and begin on a fresh journey toward self-awareness and new goal-setting.

Derail unsettling thoughts

During my times of stress, my father knew exactly how to settle me down. His method went like this: *Alright now. Catch your breath and take a calm pill. What good is your crying and carrying on going to do? Let's think about something else...* and so would come a story about the time he stitched up Pat, the family's pet cow, with his mother's quilting needle after Pat cut her neck and was bleeding too fast to wait on the veterinarian to arrive, or the time he talked a pilot through a tough landing on a plane he had engineered. Dad's stories were illustrative, plot-rich and detail-thick. Like most Aspies, he thought in pictures, and he could use that talent to draw me away from the current thoughts racing through my head toward sure disaster if they weren't derailed. His stories were always gender neutral, never condescending and always ended on a moral high road. Dad mastered the story-telling art in the way generations before any of us had. As a reading specialist and psycholinguistic and mother of three I have to say, sometimes story-telling is the best antidote to a sour mood. There are plenty of great storytellers on tape, and the radio you can turn to, should you not have a storyteller in your family or among your friends. And if you are a good storyteller yourself, I encourage you to put your stories on tape and share them with others in need of derailing or simple entertainment.

List your good stuff

Too often females on the spectrum battle with depression that comes with poor self-esteem. Raise your sense of self with a list that includes what you define as your good stuff. My good stuff is everything from the time I mountain biked by myself down a patch of the Rocky Mountains in Colorado, to the time I published my first book, to the time I made a crying baby in the supermarket smile. To me, good stuff equals anything that did the tiniest bit of good, or brought me the tiniest bit of joy, or showed me I can do something I did not think possible. Everyone has good stuff. Find reasons to be proud of who you are and what you have accomplished. If you quit biting your nails for two weeks and that was extremely difficult for you to do, put it on the list. If you showed integrity under pressure, write it on the list. If you finally learned how to tie your own shoes at 25, write it down. Remember, this list is not meant to challenge you to do things unusual or spectacular. It is merely a visual reminder that says *Yay for you!*

Stimming

Stimming is common for people with AS. It is self-soothing and calming. Chinese mind-body therapy tells us rubbing our hands together as if we are applying lotion to our palms, releases the flow of chi (energy) and chi is believed to absorb anxiety and relax the soul. If you do not already stim, or if you have another stim that doesn't seem to be calming you as much as you would like, I encourage you to release your chi.

Tapping

Tapping is a form of acupressure that is thought to free up your chi or mental energy. And the good news is, it is a very inconspicuous way to try and ease your stress and depression. When performed subtly, it just looks like you are trying to remember something or are making a gentle fidget. Using the tips of your index and middle fingers at the same time, firmly tap the areas on the bone outside the corner of one eye and then the other, at the small area between your top lip and the bottom of your nose, and on the point between the middle of your bottom lip and your chin.

The "I am" collage

Create a visual reminder of the person you are, or endeavor to be. Simply fill a poster board with things that inspire you to remember your strengths, positive traits and hopes for the future. Use anything you like to fill your board. My board contains, among other things, a piece of heather reminding me of my beloved Scottish grandmother, the first Aspie we can identify in our family; a few of my father's favorite life quotes I printed on different colored paper; photos of my children; random words that inspire me; and a variety of other personal mementoes that remind me my place in this world is something for me to cherish.

Chapter 5

Out and About

Or Traveling To and Fro

Saint Augustine once said, "The world is a book, and those who do not travel read only a page." Well, if you're an Aspie, travel is not just merely a page, but more like a huge textbook. After all, traveling presents us with numerous challenges: nerve-wracking security procedures, sensory overload, exhausting flights, extreme changes in routine, and sometimes scary or even dangerous situations. Despite all of these obstacles, to deprive yourself of traveling is also to deprive yourself of many great joys.

One of those great joys is the chance to experience the world of a different culture, and there is no doubt that traveling may reward you with some of your most treasured moments of human interaction.

The most mind-blowing act of kindness occurred to me recently during a trip to Costa Rica. My husband and I had gotten into a car accident on the winding roads, and while four men were screaming at my husband in a language he didn't know, I worked myself into meltdown mode. I sat alone in the car, crying and rocking back and forth, lost in the fear that things were out of control.

A Costa Rican woman crossed the street after a few minutes, and signed for me to open the car door, so I did. She didn't speak or understand a word of English, but that didn't seem to matter to her. She began caressing my arms and murmuring, over and over, "¡Tranquila!" My limited Spanish knew she was telling me to calm down, and somehow, I distinctly understood that she was also telling me that everything was going to be OK, that things were being taken care of. She stayed with me until the ambulance arrived, seemingly at the same time as the police and car rental company.

To my surprise, the Costa Rican man who had been in the other car, and had obviously injured his head, brought the ambulance over to me first, looking very concerned about me. Another act of kindness. Later on, I found out a man had helped my husband with translating and finding a phone to call the accident in.

As human beings, even as Aspies, we need to connect with others, and in doing so we only benefit. That benefit might occur from learning more about socializing, or from collecting the beautiful handmade arts and crafts of another culture, or from the human interaction itself.

I see her face in my mind always, and I will never forget the precious moment shared between the amazingly kind Costa Rican woman and I. And that, as experiences go, is a lottery winner.

—Annette Stanton-Harkness

I was in luck. The sign read: *Stand here for shuttle pick up.* I had just started traveling by myself and clear directions were just what I needed to keep myself safe and my nerves quiet. Literal minded though I am, I knew "stand here" didn't mean I had to actually stand at attention while waiting for the shuttle, though the thought did occur to me that if I sat down, the shuttle driver might not see he had a passenger waiting for him. Thinking I was oh so clever at having decoded the real intent of the sign, I plopped myself on the top of my suitcase, only standing up when I saw a shuttle service making its way to the pick-up spot.

Sit, stand. Sit, stand. That's what I did for well over an hour. Shuttle after shuttle came and went. A few of the drivers tossed me a wave, but not one shuttle pulled over to pick me up. I must have re-read the *Stand here for shuttle pick up* sign a few dozen times trying to figure out what the heck I was missing, or perhaps—what I was doing that kept me from being picked up. Doing a little Aspie analysis, I wondered—was this a female thing? Did the drivers think a female might not be a good tipper, so rather than waste their time on the likes of me, they'd pass by and let another shuttle driver have my business? Was it because I was a party of one, and there was some rule the shuttle couldn't stop until there were enough customers to fill the van? Did I look crazy standing and sitting, waving and talking to myself? What was the deal?

Being no dummy, I did consider finding a different shuttle stand, but with my history of getting lost I felt safer staying put just like the sign told me to. But the real reason I didn't move was because I am just plain

Aspie dogged. By God, if that sign said stand here for shuttle pick up, I would do it and I would be picked up!

During my never-ending wait, I kept seeing the same airport attendants walking back and forth to catch a smoke or some fresh air. One woman in particular was always kind enough to pass me a smile and a short *Hey, how ya doing?* Finally, the lady, probably wondering if I was zoned out on motion sickness meds or a foreigner to the States, asked me if I needed some sort of help. When I explained to her I was just waiting for the shuttle to arrive, she smiled and asked if the hotel had given me a pick-up time for its arrival. I told her I didn't realize I was supposed to call a hotel to come get me, especially since the sign didn't give those instructions. Thankfully, the lady continued her kindness, and asked me what hotel I had reserved and then she called the hotel and told them to come pick up their wayward guest. Part of me would like to say I can see where I made the mistake and that I should have known to call the hotel myself, but truthfully—I blame the sign for not being explicitly clear. It should not have assumed everyone from everywhere would understand the shuttle/hotel protocol. Yet another thing I don't understand about NT life. How in the world do people understand unspoken intent and directions? Anyway... I thanked the lady and tossed off my naivety by telling her I was not used to an airport as large as this one in Los Angeles. She laughed the whole thing off and soon enough the shuttle arrived. I gave the driver the name of my hotel and tuned my MP3 player to the relaxing stuff I needed to almost nap. The drive seemed to take forever, but hey, that was to be expected in Los Angeles. Traffic, road detours, distance between here and there, those are nothing to the big city folks. We got to my hotel about 30 songs later. I made sure to give the driver a manly tip and could almost feel the cush of my hotel bed beneath my aching back as I made my way to the front desk. I needed a lie down and fast. An Aspie's nerves can only stay flexible for so long and mine were jumping around like raindrops on a pond.

Minutes turned to moments as the desk clerk searched for my name. My double surname can cause a problem, so at first I wasn't all that surprised. But when he finally came back to tell me there was no reservation under either Holliday, Willey or Holliday Willey, I started to have that oh-crap-not-again moment of terror that screams *Mistake, mistake, mistake has been made!*

I don't understand, I said. *How about you tell me where the autism conference is setting up, and I'll get them to help us.* Wasn't that clever of me?!? Yep, then imagine my surprise when the clerk told me the hotel wasn't hosting an autism conference. Nerves starting to ripple, I took out my note pad and told the man he had to be mistaken, that my notes clearly said I was to go to the Sheraton in Santa Monica. *Lady*, he couldn't help but smile as he said, *you're in Santa Ana.*

If only I could say this was the last time I ever experienced a glitch in one of my trips. Alas, it took me several years and who knows how many miles, to teach me the real nuts and bolts of travel. And boy, are there a lot, especially in the post-9/11 world. Nothing is consistent about travel now. Every airport, travel station, bus station and travel association has his or her own rules and rituals that change with the wind. I try to keep up with the changes, but it doesn't do me a whole lot of good because the people in charge of the changes don't seem to realize they have an obligation to quit making up new rules as they go.

I've discovered that to travel safely, you have to travel composedly. Composure is not the first adjective that comes to mind when the concept of AS is considered. As much as it upsets me to say this, there are many in this world who view people with differences as disabled, crazy or downright frightening. We've all seen the fleeting glances and the stares that all but shout, *What a weirdo.* In this high alert era "weird" takes on a whole new meaning elevating the semantics from odd to possible security threat. Just last week I was detained because I was unable to handle the new full-body scans at the airport security, without having a mild meltdown. I thought I was pretty composed, but the security guard didn't agree. She heard me talking to myself and must have read my body language to mean crazy alert, instead of lady who was trying to keep herself calm and quiet when all she really wanted to do was give a loud rant about the many reasons behind her disdain for the full-body scan! The agent kept asking me what was wrong and instead of giving her my long list of complaints, I decided to tell her I was claustrophobic, which isn't a lie, but wasn't the whole truth. The agent was nice enough, but rather condescending and suspicious. After going through the stupid body scan, I was treated to a pat down that almost did me in. This kind of agent twice-over security happens to me (and many of my Aspie friends) frequently. When we travel it is so important to focus on remaining calm or *tranquila*, just as the Costa Rican woman taught Annette in the intro to this chapter.

A few years ago I found myself with a long layover on the last leg of a trip. Trying to make the best of the layover and my mind off the fact that I hated air travel, I took out an art kit I keep filled with lots of stimmy beads and clasps and little tools (airline approved, of course) for jewelry making. A Spanish-speaking couple sat next to me and we played with each other's language trying to share ideas on what beads might make up into a lovely bracelet. All was going so softly. This layover was actually rather pleasant. And then… a call came over the intercom asking for a Lion Whylee. I laughed a bit at the name, wondering who in the world would name their child Lion. Again and again the name was called until it finally dawned on me this was another case of my name being mispronounced. That feeling of chest tightness and distress found me quick, and walking up to the attendant's counter, I knew I was about to hear some news I wouldn't like. All I clearly remember is the airline attendant saying, *Miss Whylee, you're being bumped to a later flight that will take you to Chicago and then to Detroit and then to your final destination. Here's your new…* That was all I needed to hear before I began to chant *ADA. ADA. Americans with Disabilities Act. ADA.* As you might imagine, this did not get me very far. *Miss Whylee, what are you saying? Take your ticket and come back when your new flight arrives.* Nope. I wasn't having it. *ADA. ADA.* I could hear myself speaking, chanting and freaking out and I couldn't stop it. I saw a man out of the corner of my eye come to the counter and speak to the airline attendant. She gave him what I took to mean an impatient look as he talked to her, but no matter her non-verbal message, she listened and nodded her head first at him and then at me. The man came over to me and spoke so gently I knew him to be a kind spirit. He asked me what I needed and I said, clipping my words to get them out quicker, *I have Asperger syndrome and I cannot take a bunch more flights before getting home. I'm tired. I've been traveling all weekend and this doesn't make sense. Why am I being bumped? I didn't do anything wrong. I don't get it. Seriously, I won't be able to handle more airports and more getting lost in those airports and more waiting and you know what, if they bump me I probably won't even make it home tonight because my little airport doesn't have a lot of flights in and out of there. This is all just stupid and so why in the world is this happening…* and so I rambled until the man, an attorney it turns out, told me to calm down and listen to him. He would go speak to the attendant and explain it would be a really bad idea to bump me from the plane. He told me he would use the ADA defense and not only that, he'd walk on the plane with me to make sure I was OK. This guy was the best gift I had gotten in months! Sure enough, he worked his magic legal mumbo-jumbo on the attendant because a few minutes after he spoke to her, she called me up to her desk again, this time with different new. *Lady*, she said, *I don't know what you got, but you can get on the plane.* Yes. I was in. *But wait*, I asked. *Do you want me to board the plane now? Do you mean in a few minutes? Or do you mean when you call everyone else to the get on?* The deer in the headlights look flashing above my head must have been blinking brightly because while the attendant just stared at me like I was the nut she knew me to be, the attorney came to my aid and said, *Come on. She means we can board now.* And so I did, with the attorney following close behind. On the plane I couldn't help but smile, finally calm and relaxed. Thinking back on the whole thing, the situation was never as bad as I thought it would be when I was panicking. I would have gotten home if not that night then surely the next morning. I had a nice visit with a nice couple from a culture different from mine. I met a Good Samaritan. And let's face it, the name Lion Whylee is pretty darn funny!

It helps me to remember, though getting to and fro might be a drag, the result of travel can be a very good thing because it leads to new adventure, new background knowledge and new socializing opportunities, if we take care in where we go and how we get there.

~

Several years ago I bought a really neat bike for my birthday. It can handle all kinds of roads from mud to gravel to grass. I love the bike and I spent a decent sum of money on it, knowing it would be way cheaper in the long run to ride my bike around town than to drive my car. My town boasts a fabulous bike trail that links several towns throughout the local region. It's an award-winning trail with great pavement and loads of shade trees. It is a very straightforward no-way-to-get-lost trail with explicit signage indicating where cars will cross, where drop-offs in the topography are or where town limits begin and end. My plan was to get the bike and make the trail my highway. Nice plans that never came to be. It scares me to take a long all-alone bike ride on the trail. My mind wanders to kidnappers, to falls with no one around to hear me crying over a broken bone and to the inevitable flat tires. What should be an easy trip from one town to another quickly turns to something overwhelming, almost as overwhelming as travel on mass transit.

I have taken mass transit in all sorts of shapes and sizes. I've taken it in Amsterdam, Australia, New York, Chicago, San Francisco, Mexico and places in between with nary a problem I couldn't fix; yet, I am not a fan.

I hate the sounds, the smells, the robotic voices telling you what town you are in and the anxiety over what might happen if I miss my stop. Mostly, I dislike the crowds and the awkwardness of sitting or standing by strangers. Are you supposed to talk to the person next to you? Can you comment on their clothing or the book they are reading? Is it OK to smile at their children or ask the interesting women where they get their hair styled? What about eye contact? Do you look at people in the eye, to the sides of their heads, down at the floor, over their shoulder? Agh! The protocol is too mysterious for me. Mass transit is a wonderful natural resource saver, but it's hard as heck on my demeanor. If I could, I would drive my car everywhere. Now that I know how to drive well.

The first few decades of driving were no fun for me. My parents bought me a great first car I dearly loved... cleaning and admiring! I didn't much enjoy the driving part. I had a hard time judging where other cars were on the road and how close they were to me. Every time a horn sounded, I jumped and lost my place on the road. I worried other drivers weren't paying attention and would run into me no matter how diligent I was to avoid them. What a nightmare. It took getting over a few nasty car accidents and lots and lots and lots of practice to teach me how to drive without jumping through one anxious hoop after another. Now that I have mastered it, I would rather drive in my own car than use any other form of transportation. There's just one problem. I get carsick.

Traveling to and fro is both a necessary evil and the means to what can be a great experience. That's what I tell myself every time I reach for the carsick bag.

"Travel here, there and anywhere" supports

There are many fears and frustrations you can conjure up and give in to when you consider traveling, but travel can do a great many good things to women on the spectrum. I find when I am in a country different from my own, or even a state where I would clearly stick out as an outsider, I actually feel freer to be me as I am. Folks seem to blame my unique behaviors on my hometown. Fine by me. Sometimes I do not want to explain the whole AS thing or discuss my neurological needs and concerns. That having been said, it is important to consider the mores and codes of the places you'll travel to, especially if you are traveling to an area of the world where women are not thought of as the equal sex.

As an Aspie you are probably a pro at researching and/or web surfing, so use those talents to help you find out the most you can about anywhere you wish to go. Follow the golden travel rule: plan ahead. Remember, the more information you have on the places you plan to visit and the routes and ways you will travel, the calmer your jitters will be. A calmer you is a you who will be more able to prepare for the worst and plan for the best. If you're traveling locally, you can afford a few slip-ups, but if you are planning a big trip, especially one out of your own country, it is imperative you be as familiar with your destination as is possible. Here are some tips for travel.

Build your background
RESEARCH YOUR DESTINATION

Fill a scrapbook or notebook with all kinds of information about your destination including everything from maps to pictures, to what other travelers have said about the area, to the old and recent history of the place. Watch films and videos shot at the location (keeping in mind movie magic can make something look worse or better than it really is) and take notes about the colors and feel of the area. Create a feel for the place; realizing your Aspie senses will impact how an area feels.

PICK A PLACE TO STAY

I prefer hotels, knowing I could never share a room at a hostel nor enjoy the small talk held at a bed and breakfast. Wherever you choose to stay, gather photos that do a good job of illustrating where you will go. Beware that photo angles and photoshopping can alter the way a place might really appear in real life. This is particularly important to know when it comes to finding a place to stay during your trip. I recently heard a story about a man who decided to stay in a hotel because it looked so beautiful in a magazine advertisement. He barely recognized the hotel when he arrived and saw it was surrounded by a block of soot spilling power plants, a torn-up sidewalk that spreads a mile between the hotel and the train station, and nothing else, not even a broken dandelion. That's the sort of misinformation an advertising photo can provide. Look up several photos of your destinations and read non-biased reviews of the accommodations before you book your stay.

GET ALL YOUR INFORMATION IN WRITING

Write the operations directors or manager of all the places you hope to visit. Specifically ask for the daily schedules, open and closing times, the costs related to admission, and directions from the destinations to your hotel. Get everything in writing. It might all sound easy to remember at first, but as time gets closer and travel gets rolling, you might be surprised at how much you forget.

THINK ABOUT SAFETY ISSUES

Don't be shy about asking online groups and tourism associates which areas around town are safe and which are not, especially if you are in an area where you are not certain how the locals react to a woman on her own. Even if the area respects women, criminals will still see you as their first line of prey, so consider joining a tour group. I realize that if you are like me, the mere thought of being social on an already stressful event like a trip might seem paradoxical, but there are situations when it is safest to travel in packs. Learn something from our animal friends and stick to others when safety issues loom large.

DON'T FALL FOR THE NONSENSE

People who make a living off travelers and/or consumers are capable of telling you anything they think you need to hear in order to get you to purchase their wares or services. Listen to your instincts and if anything you hear sounds remotely untrue, pass on the offer and find another dealer or provider. When it comes to finding transportation support, accommodations, good shopping areas, etc. stick with the providers that come with good references such as those publicized at the airports, train stations, and by well-respected review groups. I like to follow up my references by asking people in the area what they think of the destination, but I am very careful about who I ask. I wouldn't ask a group of college kids where they are going to go to eat dinner, for example, but I might ask a group of airline personnel.

POST-9/11 SPECIAL CONCERNS

Security is making it very tough to relax and act composed. Aspies can send signals that seem to say we are frightened or worried, concerned or angry—all signals that send security in to high alert. Because you may be detained or questioned at any time during any travel from the subway station to an airline check point, do not go out unless you have a list of support people you can rely on to help you out of the sticky and scary situation. A letter from your doctor explaining the way AS affects you and a few names and numbers of people who can vouch for your good character are a must. I would go a step farther if I was traveling far away from home and put together a list of local psychologists and any legal assistants I could find through other people's reliable suggestions.

Travel buddies

I do most of my traveling alone, but I try to travel with a friend when possible. If I could, I would travel with a furry friend all the time. It is a fact animals can lower a person's blood pressure and anxiety levels. When our nerves are calm and our anxiety is low, we are naturally better suited to focus on other issues like our surroundings, social skills and essential needs. Perhaps some of the ideas below will help calm your traveling nerves.

- If you have a dog or cat you can have certified as a therapy pet, by all means travel with your pet. But realize that even a certificate by a recognized group and a doctor's letter supporting your needs might not be all you need to convince some people to let your animal stay with you at all times. Do your research and make sure your chosen means of travel and your hotel and places you wish to visit accept service animals. Get a letter from the person in charge of visitors and passengers asserting you have been given permission from them as well as your doctors and other certifying groups. And be sure and pack your animal's health records, veterinarian's contact information and all the travel goodies your animal will require.

- When you go out to a restaurant or nightclub, make certain it is a place not reserved for, or mostly catered toward, singles only. Singles spots are more apt than other places to hide dangers like date drugs and men looking for risky kinds of activities.

- If you are taking a long cross-country drive in your car, invest in a blow-up buddy you can stash in your glove box and with a flip of a switch, inflate so it looks like you have someone in your car with you. Make sure you dress up your blow-up buddy. It will make them look all the more real.

- Put on a few pretenses. Consider wearing a wedding ring, if you don't already. Pretend you are speaking to someone on the cell phone if you feel a threat or eyes watching you as you walk alone. Walk near enough to a group of people so it appears you might be with them. Even if it is obvious you are not, a criminal will not likely prey upon someone near a group of others.

Befriend the local experts

Take the opportunity to get to know some of the staff of your hotel. I like to introduce myself to as many new people charged with taking care of my stay as I can. If I'm out of the country, I make a point of giving a little token of appreciation to them. Tips always make for nice gestures. It's all about making a connection, not one you want to take too far, however. For example, meeting a staff member of a hotel and making their acquaintance is meant to help you have an extra pair of eyes in case of an emergency or to help you figure out some of the local traditions and hidden information gems. It is not to help you get a date to dinner or a friend to come to your room to watch a movie. Trust no one with your personal safety when you are on a trip. But it is never wrong to be kind to people put in legitimate business positions, hired to make your trip safer and more pleasant.

Hotel safety 101

Don't be lulled into a false sense of security when you are within your own hotel room. Even the most high priced, fabulous destination hotels can be fraught with unsafe features. This is particularly true if you are a single female traveling alone.

- Always do the minimum when moving into your new room. With the hotel management on the phone with you, check under the beds, in the closets and in the bathrooms to make sure you are alone. If someone is in there, your immediate cry for help to the person on the other end of your phone line will bring security to your aid. As soon as you know you are in the room alone, bolt the door for security. For added safety, bring a door jam wedge to put under the door where you are staying to avoid unwanted visitors who may well have duplicate keys or a master key to your room.

- Figure out the fire escape and memorize how to escape the hotel as soon as possible in case of an emergency. I have had to leave my hotel room on two separate occasions and both times I was glad I knew how to leave the hotel quickly and safely. One trip I was on the 11th floor and the walk down 11 floors was long and alarming. These days I ask for a room close to the ground floor because I feel the closer I am to the ground floor and the front desk, the safer I am.

- Keep a list of important numbers with you whenever you leave your room. Make sure you at least have the nearest hospital, embassy, transportation services, police station and hotel's numbers. It is also a good idea to have the number of a member of the area's nearest Asperger or autism organization (if there is one). If I were going somewhere too far out of my comfort zone, I would even go so far as to contact the organization and let them know I'll be in the area just in case I need to call on them for additional support for any reason.

Extra emergencies

- If you lose the ability to speak when under stress, consider wearing a MedicAlert bracelet or one that lets others know you have special issues that may interfere with your ability to communicate when anxious.

- Keep your passport and an extra copy of your passport in various locations among your person. The same goes for monies. Use a money belt, stash some money in the bottom of your shoes or pinned to the inside of your shirt or pants.

- Copy and paste your essential documents such as insurance cards, passports, driver's license, personal health alerts, emergency contacts, etc. on to a web-based email service so you can access them even if you lose every extra hard copy you bring with you.

- Calm your nerves the natural way by bringing a bit of nature with you. Such things as a small smooth stone, a pinecone, a twig or a fragrant herb might be just the oomph your mind needs to help you relax and enhance your mental and physical energies.

- Keep a flashlight, light-up keyring or book light you can turn on and keep on when you are walking near dusk or in the dark (never a great idea, but sometimes it cannot be avoided).

- Try to get a cell phone that will work wherever you go. There are many inexpensive prepaid cell phones you can purchase before leaving for a trip, and most major phone companies have some sort of international service plan you can sign up for.

Mind your Ps and Qs
KNOW YOUR AREA

When I was in Mexico I gave the ultimate respect to the locals who treated their siestas very seriously. One of the members in my party was upset there were no restaurants open to serve us lunch during siesta time, but I thought it rude to expect anyone to put aside their routines for us visitors. I travel with the idea of learning from others and with the thought that I am a lucky guest in their home, but also with the idea that if I do not follow most of the local customs, I might find myself in danger.

One trip, I woke up at 9 am ready to explore a busy city. It never dawned on me to check the local time where it was only 6 am, not a very sane time for sightseeing. The early hours are the most common hours for muggings and theft and nothing at all is open to explore even if it was safe. Pay attention to your time zones and if you have a choice, go out an hour or two after everything has opened and return home an hour or two before the places close.

DON'T DRAW ATTENTION

Do not engage in political discussions with anyone at anytime. I found myself in the middle of a heated discussion on a U.S. political policy while visiting in another country. The citizen from the other country grew angrier and angrier with me before I finally realized I was crossing some seriously dangerous lines. From now on, if I am traveling by myself or with a small group, I smile and nod even if my own country or a favorite issue of mine is being ridiculed. While on the surface this makes me feel like I'm selling out my causes or beliefs, I seriously doubt a quick conversation with a stranger with a totally different point of view than mine, would result in either of us changing our opinions. So why risk drawing attention to myself for no real benefit?

- Wear conservative clothing. Wear clothing that is culturally acceptable if you are traveling to the Middle East or any conservative or religious area where women are expected to follow a specific dress and behavior protocol.

- Beware the bling bling. Fancy jewelry, even fake jewels, can send the message you are worth a fight. Leave the glitz and glamour at home.

- Adopt a humble but confident attitude so as not to draw unwanted attention to yourself. Try not to act intimidated, lost or frightened.

Watch your step

Be very observant of your surroundings. Do not get caught up in the tiny details we Aspies are so drawn to. It took me two hours to find my way back to a hotel I was familiar with in New York City, because I kept wandering in and out of stores, making random turns and street crossings until I was blocks and blocks away from my hotel. It took real concentration to keep my mind on the business of finding my hotel and not on the sight-seeing, but I did it just before dark hit. If I had been brand new to New York, I would have had a panic attack for certain. Don't let that happen to you!

Stay away from secluded areas like car garages, alleyways and parking spaces far from the entrance to your location. Anything out of the limelight is a favorite nook for criminals. Unfortunately, public restrooms tend to be off the beaten path, so when you must use the restroom, remember to keep stall doors locked, and do not let your purse, briefcase, wallet or other personal belongings sit in a vulnerable place where a thief can snatch them while you are using the bathroom.

- Carry a walking stick or umbrella you can use as a visual deterrent or weapon if you have to. Thugs are not as interested in coming after a woman who has something she can easily use toward her defense. Criminals do not want to waste time fighting with their victims.

- If you have long hair you might want to consider wearing a hat or wig because long hair, especially braids and ponytails, make it easier for a perpetrator to grab you.

- Keep your cell phone, camera and other items you will be using on a regular basis in a place you can easily find and use them. If you become preoccupied with looking for something in your bag, you make yourself more vulnerable to someone looking to overpower a distracted female.

Pack wisely

Plan to pack several days before you are scheduled to leave. The time between when you begin planning and when you leave will give you time to re-think the items you are planning to bring, time to remember things you may have forgotten and plenty of time to be sure you've accounted for everything.

BEFORE YOU LEAVE—CHECKLIST

☐ If you are bringing your computer, back your files to a disk you will leave at home.

☐ Confirm all of your reservations.

☐ Check for any delays or detours.

☐ Tell neighbors you will be leaving, if it is for an extended period of time, so they can keep a safe eye on your property.

☐ Arrange to have your pets and plants cared for.

☐ Arrange to have your mail stopped or picked up by a friend.

WHAT TO PACK—CHECKLIST

☐ Color-coordinated clothing you can mix and match for multiple outfits

☐ Wrinkle-free clothing

☐ Socks

☐ Undergarments

☐ Sanitary hand wipes

☐ Pajamas

☐ Rain gear

☐ Work out clothing and/or swimsuit

☐ Chargers and adapters

☐ A cell phone that will work at your destination

- ☐ Several plastic bags for your liquid items
- ☐ Extra batteries
- ☐ Ear plugs
- ☐ A pillow
- ☐ Travel medications
- ☐ A mini fan
- ☐ Writing pad and pens/pencils
- ☐ A sensory ball
- ☐ Eye mask
- ☐ Water in a misting bottle
- ☐ Disinfectant wipes
- ☐ MP3 player and ear phones

Chapter 6
Body Beware

Keeping the Mind and Body Connected

A woman's relationship with her body is a mysterious and often complicated dance, all the more so for women with AS. Growing up with AS can put a woman at great risk of developing a false, incomplete, or nonexistent relationship with her physical self. Knowing your body and how it responds to various sensations, emotions, thoughts, and situations is essential for self-understanding and personal growth. This knowledge and connection to our bodies also helps to keeps us safe—what could be more important?

—Shana Nichols

The Aspie body is not your normal body. We have physiological idiosyncrasies that can boggle the mind. Take pain, for instance. While some of us are hypersensitive to pain, reacting to even a little bitty tug on a braid as if it were a machete to the back of the neck, many of us go to the other extreme and have no reaction to pain at all. I'm the no-pain kind of girl. I wasn't conscious of my high pain tolerance until after giving birth to my 9lb 7oz baby the natural way. My parents knew I was a tough cookie early on. When I was two years old I cracked my head open, but didn't shed a tear. When I was a few years older I earned the nickname "Miss Accident Waiting to Happen" because I'd come home with swollen ankles and skinned knees and knots on my head. I put a hot iron on my wrist when I was a kid just to see what it would do. I cut through my finger trying to cook a meal and my only complaint was the fact that I couldn't get the yellow gushy fat of my finger pushed back in to my skin so the bleeding would stop and I could then get back to the meal. A neighbor kid smashed my finger in between a folding chair and it was my mother, not me, who insisted I go to the doctor to see if my finger was broken.

I slid through the years not cognizant pain was supposed to sound alarms after burns and cuts and falls, but I was well aware labor and delivery would be tough. The ladies in my delivery ward knew it too. I don't think there was one lady not asking or screaming for pain medications while all I begged for was silence. My husband finding treats in his snack bag sounded like cracking walnuts and my eyes watered when the nurse turned the light on, so I knew my sensory system was wide awake. I felt the pain of my contractions, but not to the point I needed to scream for medication. And I am not averse to taking pain meds. I take them regularly for migraines and I take them immediately after surgery. I am not immune to pain. Pain just doesn't take me over. I missed all the signs that should have told me I needed gallbladder surgery and a colon resection. It took a routine ultrasound to see my gallbladder was bad and a trip to the hospital after hours and hours of vomiting before yet another ultrasound discovered my colon was dangerously close to bursting. While this may sound like I'm a lucky girl, I'm not. I can get perilously close to a life-threatening illness and not even realize it.

This inability to connect with my body in pain, presents the weirdest reality. When I am stressed too much, my body seems to evaporate. It's like my body slips into a deep meditative state while the rest of me flakes off to look around the room and take in every detail and every nuance of every thing. Then something in me clicks. When my body gets too separated from my conscious movements and thoughts, I instinctively go to desperate lengths to ground myself.

When my father died, I had this separation effect. The first thing that came to my mind was to get rid of my mind. I banged my head against the wall, slowly, rhythmically, like a basketball player dribbles a ball waiting to throw the opposition off. My consciousness was my opposition. I don't know who told me to stop hitting my head or if I just did, but the next thing I remember, a nurse asked me to sit in a wheelchair so she could take me to the chapel. I tried walking around the little labyrinth annexed to the chapel I tried praying and I tried talking myself out of my filmy orb, but I couldn't. The only thing I could think to do to reconnect was to scrape. I took a key out of my pocket and started raking it across my arm. That was better. Much better. My body started patching back to my mind. Calm. It was finding me. My mother found me doing this and, of course, it freaked her out. She saw my behavior as a sign I was losing my mind, thinking there is no other explanation for self-injurious behavior. My mom may have been right. I'm not sure. I do know that to someone like me who has hyposensitive sensory integration dysfunction, self-injury feeds the need to feel, literally and figuratively. Eventually, my mom's pleas to quit hurting myself made their way through my slippery mind and I did stop, until I was all-alone. Then I could scrape the key on my arm and put this Humpty Dumpty back together again. Truly, without a wake-up call to my sensory system, my body would have shut down. If only this were a safe way to patch things up.

I understand why girls cut. I understand why it is extremely dangerous and something we absolutely should not and cannot do. What I wish for is an alternative that works as well to elevate the emotional pain, ground our bodies and make us whole. Obviously the worry is that Aspie females will unintentionally do great harm, possibly irreconcilable harm, to their bodies when all we are trying to do is reconnect, to feel.

The lesson to be learned is simple. Anyone on the spectrum should take care in caring for her body. If you need something strong to make you connect, realize cutting and scraping things against your skin is bound to cause at least infections and scars and more than likely people's shocked attention, the kind of attention that lands you in a special room with lots of doctors knocking on your door. It's almost impossible to convince someone you aren't trying to hurt yourself when they see evidence to the contrary. I tried it. No one believed me, and that was almost unbearable. If you self-injure, be objective and make yourself believe this simple equation—*If I can see evidence of physical affliction, I am going too far*. And don't try the thought *I will cover up my cuts and then no one will know*. Sooner or later someone will see the injuries and after that there is no rewinding the scene. Professional help is needed to help you find a safe way to feel your body and to reconnect. Consider going to a physical or occupational therapist along with your counselors to figure out the best way to heal you without hurting you.

∼

Pain isn't the only "body beware" issue Aspie females face. Sadly, it is very common for Aspie females to develop eating disorders. This could be related to our obsessive-compulsive nature. It could be our innocent belief that the fashion media's message to be tiny and thin is the message we should follow. Or it could be that our sensory system freaks out when our stomach is too full, a food smells too strongly or tastes too sickening. In my case, it was a bit of a mixture of all the above.

My system demands lots of stuff, and my appetite is voracious and welcoming to most every sweet, every grain, fruit and vegetable on the planet. Meat—well, that good old thinking-in-pictures ability I have pretty much keeps the image of a cute cow or squealy piglet bled for my plate far away from my meals. Beyond those meats, all else is fair game and I love everything from the foodie rituals to the satisfaction of a full tummy, way more than most people I know. Again—Aspie behavior in extreme. I spent the first 20 years of my life gobbling my favorite goodies down until my pants squeezed my waistline too hard and I literally felt the need to puke. Which I did. Bulimia became my eating disorder because it allowed me to satisfy my desire to chew and eat, with my disdain for tight clothing. Soon enough, binging and purging had me in its camp. Such a gross thing, but even the feel of warm gushy puke on my hand didn't disgust me. The smell was tough to take, but the feeling of the gushy mess wasn't unpleasant at all. My sensory system was happy to put food in and then feel it come out. Disgusting, but true. After a short while, this became a pattern—a ritual and a routine I got rather addicted to. Of course I was always smart enough to know bulimia, along with eating disorders in general, was absolutely one of the worst things you could do to the body. I knew I was starving myself and I knew the repercussions of that. But I tell you, once a pattern is established and the sensory diet is so happy, it is damn hard to change the destructive circle. Eventually, I did manage to put an end to the bulimia, but not until it began to show up in the color of my teeth, the dullness of my hair, the pimples covering my face and the all-over feeling of sick a starving body will send out. Stopping the behavior was extremely difficult and I did it in small chunks, little by little. The crazy thing is there are plenty of times my body still feels the need to purge. I can control the feeling, but it isn't always easy.

⁓

When we put our mind to something, we will try our best to do what we set out to do. Now I am not an athletics coach, but if I were one I think I might like having an Aspie athlete on my team. I know there are plenty of people who will tell you a person with AS cannot make a good athlete, but I'm not sure why this blanket statement is so often made. When my daughter was diagnosed, we were told not to expect her to be much of an athlete. She was accident-prone like her mom, and had similar bilateral coordination and fine motor skill problems just like I did. These realities certainly make it harder for some sports to be learned. Add in the typical chaos that comes with team sports, and it is easy to see why a counselor would think an Aspie wouldn't make a good competitor. The odds might be stacked against us, but if an Aspie really wants to be good at a sport, I'd bet she can be. That doesn't mean she will be a good *team* player, though. It means she will likely give more hours of tenacious practice and more energy into her sport than a neurotypical might ever think about giving. This behavior can serve as a good role model and inspiration for others on the team. Nothing inadequate about that!

My daughter has a love for swimming and volleyball and what she lacked in athletic grace, she made up for in a commitment to practice until perfect and an astonishing amount of will power. She became the athlete on the team that would swim the long distances in a swim meet and the girl who would dive for volleyballs despite the fact it would tear up her knee or bang up her elbow. She too has an extremely high pain tolerance and never have I seen her cry or complain over the many bruises her body takes on. Still, I imagine she will feel the residual effects of the rigors she put her body through when she is older. I know this first hand. I am not as athletic as my daughter, but I have extra strong large muscles for a female. This lets me do well in horseback riding, skiing, biking and other events that tap into large muscle movements that don't demand lots of bilateral coordination. But man oh man am I feeling the after-effects of too much pounding on my system! Despite my high pain tolerance, arthritis has gotten the best of my neck, both of my rotator cuffs and the meniscus in both of my knees. Years of not even knowing I was abusing my body for the simple sports I craved have surely caught up with me.

My body might be telling me it is beat up now, but I am still a lover of all things gymnasium-related. The smell of sweat, the atmosphere of intense concentration, the sounds of weight plates cling-clanging on the iron bars and people slow groaning to press one more pound or run one more lap, feed me well.

During my disaster-filled college years, the university's gym was one of the places I could go to and be myself. The weight room was on top of the floor gym so getting to it was half the fun. Its stairs were tucked in a dark corner a novice gym user would miss if she weren't on the look out for them. There was no sign announcing where they went but having no fear of architecture and the hidden gems they might be holding, I had no trepidation climbing those stairs the first time I saw them. When I saw the secret society of jocks pouring their everything into their passion for lifting weights, I knew I had discovered something special. To my relief, no one turned to greet me or make a fuss, as had been my experience when I tried my body in the fashionable and girl giggly aerobic dance class. The weight room had no talking, no fluffs, and no fashion show. Just hard muscle work and serious business. Weightlifting fed my sensory diet the information it craved and the all-business attitude led overwhelmingly by men and machines, made a very nice fit for me.

Men. I adore them. They have always been easier for me to get along with than women. I think the male brain is similar to the female Aspie's brain in all the right ways. I find men to be more logical, practical, forthright and unemotional than women. As an added bonus, it seems a whole lot harder to hurt their feelings, which makes my bluntness nothing I need to hide when I am around them. Working out with guys and weights made me feel securely attached to the world. It was a great experience until I overdid it. The guys weren't stressing me out with social prowess skills but their love of weights brought a different kind of pressure. Their intoxication with weights caught me full on, not letting go until I too wanted to lift heavier and heavier weights while never bothering to consider proper form or my personal limitations. Looking back, I know I was only a year or so into the game before the payout began to take its toll on my knees, neck and shoulders. I remain friends with a few guys from the gym, and, like me, their bodies are paying for hitting the weights too hard too often. Thank goodness like me, they have high pain tolerances! Many are the days I wonder just how much longer even I can work through the destruction I've done to my major body parts.

On balance, the weight room was a sweet complement to my perseverating, sensory needs and social safety zone, so for now I can take the cracking knees and shoulder surgeries in stride. I wish I could find another activity that would bring back that same sense of good community. I wish the gym had been the only social scene I relied on in my early 20s. In my case, working out, no matter the hurt it brought to my body, was far safer than the hurt my drug abuse brought.

~

During college, drugs were my date to social events. Without them, I didn't have the nerve to attend. I spent years and years feeling desperately guilty over my use of illegal drugs. Then Tony Attwood set my guilt packing. He pointed out I was not so much a person abusing drugs, as I was a person trying to self-medicate my way to a life I could manage. That message, if misconstrued, could sound like I am saying it was OK for me to smoke pot and drink when I was underage. There is never any excuse for taking an illegal substance or for relying on it to make a day go better. What I am trying to say is that my reason for doping was to feel normal, not to be cool getting high or impress friends at a keg party. Sadly, my fellow partygoers didn't know this. They were oddly impressed by my ability to smoke so much pot. It was a weird time in our history. Pot was popular and so were the people who used it. How ironic that the very thing I needed to keep my nerves low enough to attend a party was the very thing that would make me the hit of the party. I don't know why I was able to take in so much pot without passing out or going crazy. In perfect irony, my experience with marijuana saved me and hurt me at the same time. It was my ticket in, but it trapped me in a world that wasn't self-directed. I became a different person when under the influence. That person had many likeable traits, but the nice traits were superficial. When the pot wore off, I was the same person I had been before, and that person had no idea how to turn on and turn off the charm and people skills without the help of a drug.

I met a fantastic man while in college and with his attention and care, the pot became a distant memory. He was a sweaty athlete who shared the laid-back attitude of low socializing, lots of good eating and roughhouse wrestling for fun. I wish I could have come out of my shell and learned how to deal with people and places all on my own, but I am thankful this friend was attracted to me just as I was, no changes needed. His confidence in me gave me the courage to design new coping strategies that fit my personality first and society's expectations second. Thanks in large measure to him, I could look in the mirror and not hate what I saw. He brought me back to a personal comfort zone the harsh realities of life in college had crushed. With him by my side I had an unbelievable amount of self-worth restored. Maybe it was the dopamine love can give you. Maybe it was just a good solid friendship that every human being deserves. Whatever it was, my times with this person represent for me the truth that under the right circumstances and with the right caring person I can be happy and free in me.

We talk so much about social skills and behavior issues when we discuss AS. They are essential pieces to our whole, but I look forward to the day more discussion bubbles up around our bodies, our brains, our ability to connect the two and the pathways to finding someone or something to help us along our way. Now that is a solid Aspie female worthy quest!

"Body and mind awareness" supports
Pain

It is essential you tell your physicians and all first responders you have either an exceptional pain tolerance or low pain tolerance. They may not believe you at first, so a letter from a physician who can verify this truth would be good to keep in your wallet or purse. Because you might not be able to trust your body's signals, it will be very hard to discern for yourself if something is really hurt or not. Objective medical tests and an observant caregiver will be your best allies in a defense against a broken body. Objectives tests could include:

- sexually transmitted disease/pregnancy/HIV tests
- thermometer
- alcohol breathalyzer (to measure blood alcohol levels)
- blood pressure cuff
- eye chart (to measure vision changes that could implicate a migraine, aneurism, torn retina, etc.)
- weight scale
- breast self-exam kit
- stethoscope.

Beyond the tests and kits meant to keep you safe, become a regular observer of your own body. Look for changes in or new appearances of:

- bruises

- cuts

- swollen body parts

- your bowel habits

- your monthly reproductive cycle

- warts and moles

- the color of your urine

- vision problems

- hair growth.

Risky activities

Bad enough I cannot tell when my body is infected or under siege, super bad I add to the risk of illness and injury by taking part in physical things that have a high risk. Aspies tend not to think in terms of consequence, especially when there is something we really want to experience, such as skydiving or rock climbing. When you factor in our coordination and balance problems it becomes clear, risky behaviors need to be balanced by extra safety measures or put on a list titled *No matter how keen I am to do this adventure, I will not unless I am with an expert in the field to guide me.* If you are unsure of the risks of your sport or adventure, do your research to find out.

Make it a point to go over the risks you want to take but really should not. Make substitutes that will come close to the real thing. Find something totally different to satisfy your craving for the adventure. For example, I love riding horses and had many fun years of jumping them and riding them bareback over crazy terrain and into lonely areas. Many falls, ligament tears and a few trips to the hospital finally made me realize I could still ride, but should really take caution when jumping. Now I never ride without a saddle and I lowered the level of my jumps and took to jumping only once in a while and never without someone with me to help me remember the bits and pieces of proper form and safety. Most activities have a second safer choice. Explore your interests and take the safer option.

Eating issues
EXPANDING YOUR DIET

Wishing and forcing a change on your eating behaviors will only make matters worse. Develop a plan for eating or for changing your eating behaviors that is reasonable and not too hurried.

If you or your health care providers feel you need to expand your food choices:

- Gradually introduce a new food to your diet, striving to keep its most offensive trait hidden. For example, if you hate the way a particular vegetable smells when it is cooked, try it raw or juiced. Take just a tiny bite or little sip, keeping a neutral or cleansing taste treat ready to go to if you feel the urge to spit the newly introduced food out. Repeat the procedure if you can, but be sure to stop before the urge to vomit or the feeling of being seriously repelled overcomes you. Maybe one taste a day or every other day or even once a week is all you should shoot for. Be patient. There is no rushing this process.

- Try hiding the food in a more complex dish. For example, cooked cauliflower mashed in to potatoes is virtually impossible to taste. The two ingredients join as one. If you cannot stand the smell of the cooking cauliflower, have someone else prepare this meal for you and bring it you when you are ready to heat up. If even knowing the offensive food is hidden in your diet freaks you out, but you are willing to try and change your eating habits, get a friend to cook the new dishes for you and bring them to you so you don't have to picture the food you're trying to learn to eat as you begin eating it.

- Pay attention to all your senses when trying new things. You may have a relationship formed between say, eating a certain food or texture and an irritating sound or smell. I know when I am at a certain fast food chain, I can barely eat there because once upon a time I worked there and the visions of my taking trash out to the disgustingly rancid smelling garbage bin are enough to make me not want any of the food. Oddly enough, if someone brings me the food or I go through the drive through, I can eat the food and enjoy it very much.

- Seek the advice of an occupational therapist to be certain you are not suffering from a palate disorder or other physical restriction that makes swallowing or chewing uncomfortable or confusing.

- Establish an eating routine. I, for example, do not like mixing my food and I prefer to eat one thing at a time. If this means I have to have three plates for each meal to keep things apart and easy to reference, then I get three plates. No big deal.

- Eat alone if seeing other people chew, or hearing other people swallow, or stir their plate with their silverware, is too annoying to handle. Make things easy on yourself when it comes to something as essential as good eating habits. Once you have a positive and solid eating behavior down strong, then you can begin to try and reshape it to include a wider range of options like eating at a table with others, or going to a restaurant or party.

NUTRITION IN GENERAL

- Be aware of your body's hydration. Parched lips, dizziness, thirst, dry skin, dark-colored urine, headaches and lethargy are common reactions to a dehydrated body. And if left unattended, dehydration can lead to many health problems, even death.

- Take your multivitamins in any form you can tolerate. I like gummy bear vitamins, but can easily swallow the tablets, too. You should be able to find drops, vitamin waters and juices and dissolvable vitamin tablets at your grocery store. Experiment to find what works best for you.

- Keep a chart recording what you eat and then analyze it against your doctor's daily recommendations for food intake. Analyze what is missing from your diet and try to add it when possible. Analyze what you are getting too much of and try to slowly take that item out of your daily diet.

- Check with your physician about the possibility you have a gastrointestinal disorder or food allergy/intolerance. I am unable to eat dairy products. Many people on the spectrum report success with nutrition when they go on a gluten-free and/or casein-free diet. Note—please check with a nutritionist or physician when you make big changes to your diet.

Chapter 7

What's Looks Got to Do with It?

More Than I Like to Admit

Am I too fat or too thin?
Am I too made up for work?
Am I dressed okay for the party?
Will I be judged "normal" or "unique" in the carpool line?
That sweater is itchy, that face cream smells disgusting, that color hurts
  my eyes.
Look at that pretty girl—the put-together woman—the self-confident
  friend.
Oh, the worries, the self-doubt, the "who cares?"
Yet the senses…oh, the senses…
The conventional perception of acceptable appearances, especially for
  a girl.

—Jennifer Hendrick

Just last week my mother was facing a very dangerous surgery. The day before she was to head to the hospital, she took me to a beauty shop, sat me in a stylist's chair and said to the hairdresser, *Make her look good.* A head-full of highlights and a new haircut later, I was a trendier lady. This may sound shallow or insulting to some, but not to me. It's a life-long part of who my mom and I are; the pea being groomed by the pod. Mom always knew how to lead me to the water of beauty where I inevitably drink because—well, because some things never change…

$\sim$

Every August my mother and I would take a girls' day to get me ready for the upcoming school year. We'd get my health checked, eat a fun lunch and go shopping for my school clothes. I liked my very tall Aspieish doctor, loved his deep monotone and astute attention to detail and naturally, his pragmatic advice. *Quit biting your nails. Stand up straight. Yes it's OK if you only want to eat hamburgers every day. Outsmart the bullies.* And so it would go until I was sent on my healthy way to lunch at Famous Barr for their delectable French onion soup that performed magic in my mouth every time.

So far so good on my girls' day. Too bad shopping was up next. Just the thought of finding my way through herds of styles, picking out clothing that might possibly fit without bunching or crunching something or other, touching and smelling polyesters and silken linens— Agh! Nightmare. While my mother couldn't help me avoid the sensory overloads intrinsic to mercantile apparel, her former model know-how could quickly pick out the trendiest styles. That lady could work the racks and racks of clothing like she was spreading soft butter on toast. She made it look so easy and oddly interesting, until it came time for me to try the outfits on. The sales ladies set us up in cute corners of the store behind doors I would lock if I was lucky, or curtains the staff would pop their heads into if my luck was dry. Heads popping in through curtains spread wide make startle reflexes itch and twitch. No fun.

Somehow, someway, Mom managed to fill shopping bags with enough clothes to get me through the school year. So she says! I really don't remember much about the clothes themselves and I have it on good record that my style would never have made it on the mannequins at any store. My Aunt Barbara reminds me I may have had all the pretty clothes a girl could hope for, but somehow, when put in my hands, they came out mismatched and uncoordinated. *Liane*, she used to ask me just to be sure, *are you positive you want to go to school like that?* Answering that I was sure, she would smile her ever-accepting smile with her ever-giving love and say with the confidence only someone who really gets the Aspie mind can say—*Then off you go* as I left the house with my hair in a rat's nest and clothes covered in patterns and colors never meant to meet one another. With family like my Aunt Barbara in my court, I remained the Princess of Unique, never paying much attention to style and what it may mean. As long as I was comfy in my clothes, I was good to go.

～

I think styles were easier in the 70s. It spoke loudly on behalf of individuality; a great fit for Aspies in general. Fabrics and shape were slinky, soft, baggy and easy peasy anything goes. Thankfully, the feminist movement made bras an optional accessory that I was all too happy to cross off my must-have list. Halter-tops and bell-bottoms were perfect clothes to find comfort in. Hairstyles were long or short, but unkempt was fine, too. Make-up was minimal. Shoes were sloppy and slipper-like. Many hip-type American girls joined the Europeans and quit shaving. I joined those ranks. Thank God for the 70s style—that's what I say.

Individuality was coveted in my mind, in my home and in my school. My peers did not seem bent toward one appearance statement or another. There were pieces of clothing that came in vogue. Pea coats and desert boots were garments that made a statement about our generation, but that was cool by me. They were made for ease and comfort so I was lucky in this regard—I could dress cool without giving up my comfort. A win–win. I was not very aware of the big hoo hoo over clothing until I was in my second year of college. In fact, I remember learning the 2000-year-old phrase *Vestus virum reddit* (clothes make the man) in my Latin class and thinking—really? Clothes are that important to society, so important I'm reading a phrase from eons ago dedicated to the concept? It was astonishing to me, the kind of astonishment that makes an ah-ha light bulb blink in the mind. All the shopping trips with Mom, the cool teen clothing stores at the mall, and the stylistics of my girlfriends suddenly began to make sense to me. Style and personal carriage do make a statement in the NT world, about who we are, even if we don't realize it. It's profiling mixed with generalizing, stereotyping and an ability to read people, all judgment calls that remain unmindful for most of us on the spectrum.

With that note in mind, I now try to study fashion magazines and trend forward people I see in public and on TV for looks I feel comfortable making my own. Sometimes I find this endeavor fun, kind of like a scavenger hunt through boutiques, online off-price clothing sites and used clothing stores. What I don't find fun is tending to the other parts of looking good.

~

I struggle with personal hygiene on almost every plane mainly because there isn't anything fun or interesting about cleaning the body, shaving, styling the hair, fixing the fingernails, applying the creams and acne medicines, plucking the eyebrows and hairy moles, or finding the right make-up to cover my fastly falling face. I know loads of Aspie ladies who could care less about any style or personal hygiene issue and I think they are very brave and hip. Good for them. But as for me—I haven't the desire or nerve to walk out of my privacy without doing my best to camouflage my smells, unwanted marks, ruddiness and general yuckiness.

My husband tells me I am too critical of myself and I acknowledge that might be true. But I think there is a more fundamental Aspie trait behind my self-criticism. The Aspie sharp-eyed attention to detail makes it all but impossible to not zoom in on every tiny annoying imperfection. I go nuts when my eyelashes aren't the same length, or my teeth look too yellow or my skin spots get too dark. Not because I am trying to turn back the clock of age, but because I just don't like spots and unevenness and unsymmetrical things anywhere except in an abstract painting.

I ask myself if I would be so self-critical if I wasn't a detail-bound Aspie. I would probably buck the NT culture's rules filled with so many odd expectations and traditions because when it comes right down to it, they make no logical sense! I can't understand why men in most every walk of the world get away with less attention to body than do women. There are far more unattractive men in the media than there are women. Men aren't expected to shave, but in most countries, women are. On the other hand, men can shave their heads and call it a day, but women tend to be bound to hair-dos, hair extensions, colors and cuts and waves and perms and straightening irons and a drawer full of hair gadgets. Sigh.

~

All things remaining equal, there is one personal appearance matter I do adhere to and do find difficult to ignore, no matter how tempting. Hygiene. Body smells are a no-no, anywhere, anytime. Sweat, stenchy food spices seeping through pores, nasty rancid breath, oily hair odor, and moldy cheese smelly feet are the certain ingredients for sensory freak-outs. Some people swear they do not notice their own smells, but I find that impossible to believe. Then again, I have extra powerful olfactory skills. Still—really? Is it really possible for someone to not note her personal body odors? I doubt it.

Sensory issues will often make it challenging for an Aspie to take care of total body washes. There is a sensory response and balance issue that often overcomes people on the spectrum when water hits the head or runs into the eyes and ears. The water aside, bathing products typically contain combinations of scents and chemicals that can be very overpowering to the Aspie. Water alone is better than nothing, but in truth, it won't do much to do a deep cleanse nor much to keep skin from breaking out and drying up. Quite a conundrum, especially when the menstrual cycle starts.

Until I had a hysterectomy in my early thirties, I had bloody britches with every period thanks to abnormal uterine bleeding and a propensity to forget it was necessary to change Tampax and a refusal to wear pads that felt like someone was giving me a never-ending wedgie. I get how difficult it is for young girls, old girls and every girl in between to deal with her period. It's an ugly, smelly, cumbersome, frequently embarrassing reality for females. Imagine how much more nasty it is if you are an Aspie female with poor executive functioning skills. Lucky for me, I had a few understanding female friends and a good school nurse who were ever able to bail me out of trouble when I would discover I'd left a red blotch on my seat. The sheer mortification of those memories is startling to me even now.

One holiday while doing my best to make a sweet first impression on my boyfriend's family, I stood up from the white carpet stairs I had been sitting on only to notice my white pants and the white carpet were covered in red. I will never forget the humiliation I felt when I saw my boyfriend's brother staring at me, then the carpet, then me. He tried to smile, but it was in vain. Nothing would make either of us feel less awkward and nothing at all would make me feel better. I was too freaked out to get anyone to help me clean up the mess, too agitated to take responsibility or laugh it off. Instead, I put my coat on and got my boyfriend to get me the heck out of there. I'm not sure why I never learned to take the precautions I obviously needed during my periods, but I surely wish I had. I think the executive functioning skills were just too weak to plan ahead or have contingency plans beyond turning to a friend or the school nurse.

This chapter makes only a simple statement. Appearances and personal hygiene do matter to others, so much so that they are worth paying attention to. In many instances, they are equally, if not more, important to those of us who notice the tiny details and slightest smells. While part of my message is simply the importance of using style to make a good impression on those we need to, I cannot write that I think we should sell out our personalities just to fit in. But I can say I think it's cool and brave to learn how to be flexible enough to try on new trends and styles, particularly if something as simple as how we present ourselves gets us something we want or need like a job, the attention of someone we wish to get to know, or less ridicule by an often times overly judgmental society.

Look, it is befuddling to live in a culture filled with style contradictions and restrictions, a world where a man in a lovely evening dress would very likely be targeted by bullies and a woman with bear-hairy legs would be laughed at, a world where men can stink of sweat and be called athletes but a woman smelling of blood isn't revered as a giver of life but rather a dirty skank. But it is what it is. I suppose the best advice I can give is the following advice my mom gave me long ago... Use appearance to your benefit. Use style to send a message, use it to hide any flaws you don't like to look at. Most of all, use it to make you feel like you are the woman you see yourself being, for at the end of the debate, you have to be happy in your own skin.

"Personal clean up and care" supports
Style in the wardrobe

Style. What a nightmare for so many of us. Not only is it difficult to find and purchase an appropriate and kind-to-the-body wardrobe, it is downright expensive. I enjoy finding clothing and accessories at discount places, loving the mission like it's a game, but in truth it is my fashionista kids who keep my style on at least a passable mark. They are the people who keep the clothes in my closet from becoming too crazy for most people. If it were up to me, I'd wear nothing but my pajamas all day, every day. Not a great look when you're heading in for work. Not everyone has kids or sponsors to help them with their wardrobe, so here are some style ideas I have learned from my girls, my mom and others or just worked out for myself.

EASY ENOUGH WARDROBE BASICS

Rely on the easy classics:

- white button down shirt
- pullover or button up sweater
- pair of khaki-colored pants or skirt
- pair of black-colored pants or skirt
- simple black dress
- black or navy blazer
- two pairs of shorts, one for a dressy day out and one for casual days or relaxing around the house
- pair of chinos
- pair of blue jeans
- a few casual t-shirts and a few nicer button-ups or pullovers to wear with your shorts, jeans or chinos for work or play
- soft work-out type outfit including pants, a top and jacket to put on during fast trips out or just because you want to feel comfortable
- flat or low-heeled black shoes
- pair of casual tennis shoes.

Mix and match any of the above and that's all there is to it. Fancy? No. But always a bunch of possibilities for looks that work in play and at work, at home and for a moment or two out? Yes.

ID CARDS

If you feel more adventurous or crave more excitement than a few mix-and-match clothing items, and yet you think you might end up in things that don't go well together, lay your outfits out in groups you are positive go together (maybe you've seen them in a magazine or someone has helped you or you can manage a few mix-matches on your own) and then take pictures of the outfits. Leave the photos on the back of your closet door or somewhere you can easily access them. My daughter recently did this for her sister and the sister loves it, even though she is completely capable of making her own matches. She just likes not having to think about what to wear every morning and the photos are an easy way to avoid having to think!

UNIFORM

My mom's favorite wardrobe trick is to purchase a bunch of the same outfits in different colors once she finds one she loves. We call these her uniforms, and she loves the fact she knows she looks good in what she likes and the safety in knowing if she wears out one uniform, she has plenty of others to choose from. The only problem comes if her weight fluctuates or the uniform goes out of style before she wears them out! I'm not good on knowing when an outfit goes out of style, but an online search can help with that. Just type in a description of your outfit by the cut or fabric, and see what the style gurus have to say about it, if you too are concerned about wearing things that have passed their wear date.

COPY CAT

Rely on our ability to echo what we see and nonchalantly take in what your co-workers or neighbor ladies are wearing, before you go to pick out your clothes. While I wouldn't copy them dead on, lest I risk freaking them out or being accused of stalking them, I would note how they are dressed at work and how they are dressed when they are going out for something casual. I'd analyze their basic style recipe, for example, I'd look to see if they are wearing mostly pants and tucked in shirts, or leggings and flouncy tops, or dresses, or a variety of all the above. And I'd try to figure out where they were wearing these outfits: to work, the market, a luncheon with friends—whatever. Then I would set my norm at that.

AT HOME YOU ARE ON YOUR OWN

For sure, when I am home, I slap back on my pajamas or baggy pants and casual t-shirt. When I'm at home I do as I please, and this is how I am dressed to please when it is me I aim to please! When folks see me at home dressed like this, I make no apologies, I am who I am the moment I am not counting on a paycheck or worried about running into someone who has any influence over my life. All this sounds a bit like I'm caving in to peer pressure set by NT society, but to me this is just a pragmatic approach to living one foot in my comfort zone and one foot in a world that demands standards in return for employment or membership in whatever social club I decide is worth my time and effort.

Hair-dos

Ponytails, braids, short bobs, long straight, permed locks? Who can choose? Who wants to mess with any of them? I rely on the lady who cuts my hair to keep me from looking too shaggy-dog-like. And I always insist on a style that will happen on its own, without any more help from me than a quick blow dry with my head upside down. Someday I plan on buying a wig. My daughters have hair extensions and hairpieces they clip in to their manes to give them an instant ponytail and to hide their unwashed hair. They love their wigs and no one can tell when they have one on. Perfect. I think the only stipulation stylists recommend is the wig be made of human hair. Watch for them to go on sale at cosmetic stores and beauty shops, otherwise they could get expensive. Or find your favorite cut that you can manage and have no fear sticking to it until you feel it is time for an update.

Simple clean

Sensory nightmare. That's how I used to describe a trip to the personal hygiene aisle at the market. Thankfully, the consumer market and old-school natural recipes are turning a new page in cleaning and care options. Nowadays there are a host of virtually chemical-free products typically marketed for infant and toddler care, as well as deodorants and powders made from healthier, virtually scent-free organic options. Visit a natural health food store or look online in vegetarian and wellness sites for these products. Or if you're really adventurous or want total control over your product's consistency and scent, experiment with making your own or using what's around the house or in nature. Try these recipes out if they suit your fancy.

FLORAL SPLASH

1. Place 1 packed cup of rose petals, orange blossoms or a fragrant flower petal of your choice in a large plastic or glass bowl.

2. Pour 2 cups of boiling water into the bowl over the petals.

3. Cover and let steep for several hours or until the liquid is cool to the touch.

4. Strain the liquid into a sterilized jar.

5. Refrigerate and use within 5–7 days.

CUCUMBER SPLASH

1. Slice a large, fresh cucumber into a large bowl.
2. Pour 2 cups of cold water over the cucumber.
3. Cover and store the mixture in the refrigerator overnight.
4. Safe to use for 2–3 days.

HOMEMADE ANTI-PERSPIRANT

1. Put ½ cup of baking soda into a sterilized jar or container.
2. Add ½ cup of cornstarch.
3. Add a handful of flower petals, your favorite dried herbs (use the whole herb if possible, not ground up or processed herbs).
4. Seal the container and store in the refrigerator, shaking the mix every time you use it.

DRY BODY POWDER OR SHAMPOO

1. Put 1 cup of rice flour into a large sterilized jar or container.
2. Add ½ cup of cornstarch.
3. Add a handful of orange peels, lemon peels and lime peels; or a cotton ball sprinkled to the extent you like, in your favorite essential oil.
4. Seal the container and sit it in a cool dark place for 7 days. Shake the container every day or so to help the ingredients absorb one another.

QUICK-DRY SHAMPOOS

1. Sprinkle a handful of cornstarch, baby powder or cocoa powder (if you have brown hair).
2. Gently blend the products into your hair.
3. Let the products do their trick and absorb the dirt and grease in your hair, for 3–5 minutes.
4. Brush out the residue.

MOUTHWASH

1. Boil 4 cups of water.

2. Add a combination of the below ingredients, or any other edible bits per your interest, to equal 6 teaspoons.

    ◦ 1 tsp fresh mint leaves (spearmint or peppermint work well)

    ◦ 1 tsp rosemary leaves

    ◦ 1 tsp anise seeds

    ◦ 1 tsp cloves

    ◦ a few drops of your favorite flavored oil.

3. Steep for 20–30 minutes. Store in a sterilized jar or container.

4. Keep the mix in the refrigerator where you can use it for up to 4–5 days.

Chapter 8
Living the Life Easy?

Juggling Life vs. the Urge to Run Away

In my dreams, he caresses my soul,
Satisfies my desires, and melts away the worries of the day;
Reality returns, and I wake alone, lost without his lead.
I get through the day in a state of longing—
will my Nirvana return tonight?

—Sharon Fanjer Berry

Neurotypicals use the puzzle piece to symbolize the questions they have about autism. Ironically, people on the spectrum tend to look at life as a big puzzle. I go about my business looking at the details—the puzzle pieces, if you will—with only a guess at what the completed picture might be or could be, if only I could see it clearly or put everything together within the order it best fits. Let's say, for example, I have a day in front of me that includes doing something for one of my daughters, going to the doctor's for an eye exam, meeting a client at my barn, working on an article, and calling on an elderly relative to make sure they know they are loved. When I'm cozy in my bed and everything is quiet and dark, my mind's eye can see what needs to be done. I can go through the list of to-dos and fantasize about the end of the day that will find me taking a deep relaxing breath over a nice cup of hot tea and cream, maybe cozying up to a novel, and a yummy cookie… all part of a simple and fabulous reward for having spent a day accomplishing so much. Then something bizarre happens. I get up, get dressed, and instantly feel overwhelmed. Reality hits. I'll drop my teacup the moment the boiling teapot scares me with its scream. I won't be able to find the recipe for the cookies I had planned to make. And I will realize I loaned out the novel I had been hoping to cozy up with. Suddenly the balls I had hoped to juggle for the day will be scattered all over my head while that loud little voice inside will start ranting, *Give it up. You know you suck at managing your life. Go back to bed and try again tomorrow.*

Dang that little voice! How does she know things are always la la easy in my sleepy still-in-bed world? I ought to be as smart as her and realize by now that too many extraneous variables I could never have imagined before my feet even hit the ground for the day will plop in unexpectedly. Then again, maybe it is best I wake up deaf to any insight that would throw me off my schedule before I get started. At least when I wake up optimistic, I can set some of the day's motions into good order. I begin by trying to make a schedule of how things will work best. I think in terms of routes to take, the triage of what is most important to accomplish first or for sure, and I add in a bit of extra leeway for things that might jump up and interfere, like an empty gas tank or my inability to find the tape that will secure the package that is to be mailed. I try, try and try to figure things out in an orderly fashion. I make lists and take notes, using all kinds of visual aids, like circles around the important things and highlighter pens to keep me from forgetting things, and sometimes these tricks (along with a dash of good luck) make my juggling act go off without too many dropped balls. Those are my easy days when only a few things are on the chart to be done. There just aren't enough easy days! Something always comes up. For NTs, this creates a simple readjustment of the plan. Maybe they'll call a friend to take over a chore, or maybe they will happily put one of their responsibilities off until another time. They can shrug off the desire for routine and not hear a little voice saying *No, it has to be done this way.* We Aspies are not so lucky! We are rigid and we like to have control and we do not like surprises. I cannot speak for all Aspie women, but I bet I am when I say there are many days I wake up and think—*I think it might be best if I just run away today.*

That thought, though wildly unreal on the surface, does touch people with autism at their very core. Life is overwhelming even when we aren't trying to manage it. Life comes at us fast with noises, and lights, and confusion, and people we thought we could trust who pull the rug out from under us just as we are walking on it for the first time, and self-doubt, and anxiety, and perseverations and… the list goes on and on and on. Children with ASD have a certain laissez-faire approach I find admirable in my fantasies, but very frightening in reality. Children with autism spectrum disorders as young as toddlers, simply take off when the urge strikes them. We call them "runners." These are the kids who literally unclasp the toughest locks and blocks a door can have, to run. Bright lights and water attract the kids and things like traffic and bad people do not enter their minds. In fact, according to autism safety expert Dennis Debbaudt, it is imperative parents and caregivers with high-risk kids:

> Get expert help to manage safety for chronic, dangerous wanderers. Wandering prevention, alert and search can be addressed through planning, proactive disclosure of crucial information, technology that can alert a parent or care provider when someone leaves the premises and partnerships with search and rescue professionals. (email interview, April 2010)

My parents would have been the first to contact Dennis if he had been an expert in the field back when I was a kid. I loved to bolt out of the house with no regard for personal safety or concern the family might miss me. My mom knew to look for me in the sewer wells and in the woods behind our house. I didn't go too terribly far, but even a half a block away can be too far. One of my favorite spots was in the woods just beyond my house. Way before it was cool to like vampire lore, I fancied vampires and things that go bump in the night. One of my favorite things to do was to go underground.

Without knowing they were playing into my secret fantasy, some of my guy friends carved a tunnel in the ground deep in our woods, cleverly covered with a board that marked the spot without giving away a clue for what was beneath. The boys showed me, their token female friend, where the hideout was and I vividly remember the feeling of intoxication it brought me. We had all made a pact not to go in the hole unless we were with a friend, but I knew right away I would violate that pact. I could not wait to lie in the cool, soft earth, closed off from the sun and heat and voices and other such stuff that kept me from living peacefully in my own little world of smooth calm. I spent many a moment in the secret hole until the boys eventually grew tired of the spot and turned it into an open pit they could use for burning things. I had a healthy fear of fire that kept me away from the spot after that.

I think about lying under the ground to this day, and never does it bother me to imagine rolly polly bugs and spiders, worms and ants laid beside me. I should look back and shudder, knowing now how dangerous it was to be buried alive, but I don't shudder, and that should serve as a warning to adults sharing a life with people on the spectrum... Our desire for peace—real dreamy peace—can make it easy for us to dismiss certain dangers. If it were me and I had a friend on the spectrum who felt the urge to disappear, I would make certain I knew where their disappearing place was and I'd do all I could to make certain it was fool-proof in its safety.

That feeling I could find in the ground, the simplicity, the gentle nothingness, the not having to try so hard to understand so much that went over my head, was a feeling I have never been able to find again. But it is a feeling I've tried to capture over and over and over again. It didn't always have to be vamped around a secret spot or tiny enclosure. Sometimes the urge to bolt could be tempered and plotted for.

~

I was just a kid the first time I thought about running away from home for real and not just for a reclusive moment or two. My Girl Scout troop was taking a train trip to a museum and, as luck would have it, I was reading a book about a young girl and her brother who run away to the Metropolitan Museum of Art in New York. The book, *From the Mixed-Up Files of Mrs. Basil E. Frankweiler* by E. L. Konigsburg, was the perfect catalyst for my imagination to convince my reality that I could, in fact, have a grand runaway adventure. I can't remember why I was determined to leave home. I know it wasn't because I was particularly unhappy or trying to prove a point about the woes of childhood, but I do remember loving the idea of exploring on my own in a world stuffed with things beyond my imagination. I was devoted to the idea of living out the fantasies the kids in Ms. Konigsburg's book enjoyed. Weeks before we were scheduled to take the trip, I spent many an hour planning how I would miss the train on the return trip. I saved money to get me by just in case the museum's fountain wasn't a goldmine like it had been in the book. I packed some extra clothes and snacks in my backpack. Everything about my plan made such good sense to me. I would simply miss the train going home and live in the museum for a week or so and then I'd call my parents on a pay phone and let them know where they could come pick me up. No doubt my weak theory of mind kept me from considering there were adults on the trip who would not leave without me, and parents at home who would come looking for me if they did.

I don't know why I didn't give my plan a real go when the time came, but something kept me from it. Hmm. I wonder what it was? Well, never mind. The important part of this adventure-not-taken is the desire I had to leave; a desire not reserved for little kids on the spectrum. I know plenty of adult Aspie ladies who share stories with me about the wish to live a different life, maybe even as a different person, even if only for a while. Lots of us get involved in community theater, or write plays and poetry, or get jobs that are not at all the sort of job anyone would imagine we would have. Sometimes it is lovely pretending to be someone else. Sometimes it is easier to pretend we were not so vulnerable to so much hurt and confusion. Being Aspie is exhausting. Being someone else can mean being free.

~

I was a teenager when I thought it would be grand living in a museum. I was an adult when I took a vacation to the beach all alone. Chills stand the hair up on my arms when I think how closely I flirted with danger back then… On a whim, I took off for Florida from my small town in Missouri to find adventure. One night I went into a nightclub filled with other students on holiday. Innocent enough. Not really. I managed to find a nice-looking boy who asked me to dance. We had a fun evening filled with a bit too much drink and a bit too little common sense. But I was not I. When he asked me what I did and who I was and where I was from, I told him I was from San Antonio, Texas and that my daddy was a rich oilman. I put on a southern accent and played the new me to the hilt. The guy, also from the south, never even heard through to the falseness of my accent. I guess I was pretty good at turning on the southern charm. As it happened, I entertained my new friend all evening with fake stories from my fictitious life wandering from my experience as a ballerina (in truth, I was kicked out of ballet class at five years old for hitting the little girls next to me in line) to my adventures as a beauty queen in Texas (I would never ever enter a beauty pageant). Toward the late end of the evening, the boy told me how relieved he was to have found a real girl to spend time with, someone, he said, who was honest and respectful. I broke down and confessed my lying crimes. He took it in good stride, thankfully, and with the beer all but out of our system, he walked me back to my hotel and even spent the remainder of our holiday taking me out. I never did confess my difficulties involving fitting in, finding friends, understanding the world and all other things Aspie. His kindness toward me let me forget, for a lovely period of time, that back then I was usually the girl everyone gave a raised eyebrow to and hardly ever a welcoming hand.

The Gods were watching me this trip, because if this guy had been the kind of creep that often roams the college hot spots during holidays, I might have come out of the play world a broken doll, perhaps a dead doll. In my heart, this spring-break boy will always be a bit of a hero for letting me play a part that made me happy and whole, even if for only a while. I was old enough to realize the consequences of my actions on that trip, but the pull to be seen as a normal, fun, silly person was stronger than my worries over any consequence I could imagine. The wish not to work so hard to make a friend, not to have to swim against the current to figure things out—ah, that's a dream I have all the time.

~

The level of effort it takes for an Aspie to multitask, read non-verbal messages, decode social situations and apply solid social skills is extremely taxing on the body, mind and soul. Yet, there is no way around this situation. Like most females on the spectrum, I have no option but to stand on my own two feet and tend to my life and the life of my children. Like most moms everywhere, I am the custodial parent who is expected to volunteer in the schools, shuttle the kids back and forth, do the grocery shopping and the cooking and the housekeeping, budget the family economics, and plan whatever family calendar we can all agree on. And I'm married to a man who does his fair share of family duties. I cannot imagine how hard it would be to do all these things and keep my simple sanity if I was divorced. Even if I was a single woman living with no children, I think I would find having so much to do in terms of running a life filled with anything beyond one suitcase and a hot plate, extremely taxing. If only I could find another underground hideaway.

Aspies are not wired to handle the demands of too much, too soon, too often. We are focused beings who like centering our attention on our favorite things—things that often become careers or hobbies we can enjoy more than a dog enjoys a bone. Some of the most famous and ingenious people in history were likely on the spectrum, but not because they were great at multitasking. It was their single-minded tenacity and well-stacked brainpower that brought people like Einstein, Edison, Yeats, Lloyd Wright and Newton to the stage of brilliance. Notice, however, they were not busy women managing a job, the family and/or the other rigors of a mega society's demands. They were allowed, even applauded, for their isolated devotion to their favorite interest. The same set of standards doesn't apply to females. We would never try telling a four-year-old having a meltdown that mommy is busy with her obsessive interest and will be there for him just as soon as she is finished photographing, cataloging and mounting the 50 butterfly specimens she just received in the mail from the Department of Wildlife. We would never get away with explaining to a demanding boss the real reason why we want to skip the mandated office picnic in the park is because we have just a tiny little thing called social awkwardness and the rampant anxiety that comes along with it.

Life doesn't afford too many people a lot of opportunities to do what they want at their leisure. Sure there are people who ignore the wants and needs of others, but those people are unlikely to be women granted custody of their children and women given decent jobs. There is no question about it. It is very difficult for a woman on the spectrum to balance it all without giving up something vitally important, like time for herself, a personal life of some sort, or time to sleep, unless she is one of the rare breed of Aspie females who flies solo with little regard for her family and friends. However, if the woman is a typical, caregiving Aspie who does push through the blockades and follow her interests to where they lead, she will end up tipping into a swamp filled with guilt.

Guilt has nothing good about it. It's a lousy motivator and a mean friend. Martyrdom is old school and has no place in an Aspie's life. We deal with enough self-doubt and questions about our ability to parent and befriend. Who needs that?

When there is too much on our plate it is only natural to want to chuck the plate at the wall. I venture to guess most women are spread too thin, and I bet many of us long to disappear from time to time. Therefore, I am not going to feel bad anymore for wanting to just levitate, or run, or bury myself, out of the here and now. It has taken me a long time to give myself permission to think of my own needs without feeling residual remorse. I am reminded of an old saying that in its silliness says something brilliant, If the *Momma ain't happy, ain't nobody happy*. Isn't that the truth? If we, the moms of the world (and by mom I mean women who care for anyone or anything from a person to a plant to an animal to a business agenda) aren't happy, healthy and well, then how would it be logically possible for those we care about to be happy, healthy and well? Very simple logic, but a logic so many women ignore and so many Aspie women seem unaware of.

I do not believe we can have "it all," but I do believe we can prioritize our responsibilities, including our responsibility toward ourselves, if we have the tools to help us. The support section for this chapter includes many of those ideas, but on the whole it comes down to this: When we can find ways to both see the puzzle completed and ways to put it together when it comes apart, I think we will have found the key to living life easy.

"Living the life easy" supports

Life management is an art more than a science, which might explain why Aspies have such a difficult time managing easily or completely. On the surface it would appear those of us with a logical mind have a decided advantage that should make juggling life easier rather than harder, but alas, logic only works when life is linear. Life is rarely linear. Be that as it may, this is *the* year I figure out how to manage chores, obligations, responsibilities, etc., without leaving something out or messing something up. I will not give in to the lousy executive functioning, need for routine, dislike of the unknown, misjudging the time things take, what-if-I-mess-up elements of life that make me doubt myself and come up empty handed. Toward a goal of easier living, I hope I can devote myself to the following.

Chunking

Harvard psychologist George A. Miller coined the term *chunking* in the 1950s to represent his thesis that the human memory is most efficient when information is presented in chunks, or small digestible units. This concept when applied to life management would mean we should spend a specific amount of time and energy on one problem or issue at a time rather than multitasking, which suggests we can and should try to engage in several things all at once. Chunking was the old way of doing things.

Multitasking, especially since computers came into our lives, is the today way of doing things. Try as I might, I cannot multitask. When I try to the results are confusing and never complete. Multitasking makes me, like most Aspies, wince and whimper. Rather than working my way through too much exhaustive confusion, my suggestion is this: go back to chunking. Break down tasks into small chunks you then approach and deal with one at a time. Set your schedule before you and as you look at the list, circle those things that go together, then re-write a new list outlined with like-tasks creating one "to-do" chore. For example, you might have a list of things you need to do around town, cleaning chores and things that are extra-curricular in nature. Your list could look something like this:

Around town chores	Cleaning chores	Extra-curricular activities
grocery store	clean bathroom	make signs for the bake sale
dry cleaners	vacuum floors	walk the dogs
pick up books from library	fold clothes	go swimming
		go to a park

Even if you are tempted to begin one chore before finishing another or combine chores, for example folding clothes while cooking dinner, resist the urge. My old ways would have had me making signs for the bake sale while waiting for the dry cleaners to find my clothing, folding clothes while I was cooking dinner, and cleaning the bathroom and its floor while I am using the bathroom to get ready for going out. To a chain management professional or a computer's hard drive that is the way it should be. It can be far more efficient to multitask, but the payback can be seriously painful, at least in terms of exhaustion and our tendency to be overwhelmed and short-circuited. So, why go there if you don't have to?

Stations

Aspies often hoard or come close to it. We are the queens of personifying our belongings if only because the memories attached to certain items remain so engraved on our hearts and in our minds. This tendency doesn't bode well when mixed with poor organizational skills. Perhaps you are not a hoarder, but rather a minimalist like my father was, a person who couldn't bear to have a mishmash of messes in his periphery. Organization skills might plague you just as much, as you endeavor to keep track of and organize those things you do have to keep, like tax records, bills, keys, groceries, etc. I like the idea of using stations to keep up with your stuff.

Your personal station system has to be custom made for you, but here are some ideas to get you started.

POST-IT POCKETS

You can purchase a premade post-it pocket from stationery stores or online, or make your own with cardboard stapled together in the form of a pocket securable with a magnet you can glue on. These are great for keeping mail sorted, photos handy and receipts in check.

UNDER-THE-BED STORAGE

Use bricks, specially designed bed-frame lifts or any other secure method you can think of to lift your bed off the floor so you can slide small bins or bags filled with out-of-season items, things you don't need to look at often, or something you just have no room for like shoes and coats. One trick, make the bins or bags see-thru so you can instantly recognize the contents.

OVER-THE-DOOR RACKS

I hang all sorts of things from these. Depending on which room they are in, say the bathroom—I have bags filled with face creams and cleansers, my medicine and a robe. Or if the rack is on the last door I pass before leaving the house, I have last-minute items, like a little mirror, hair spray, pocket change and an umbrella.

BASKETS

Corner baskets, stacking baskets, hanging baskets—they cannot be beat for making a mess look more like an interesting décor decision. While you won't be able to see through most baskets making fast recognition a possibility, you can use them to hide the stuff that needs to be hidden. I use them to stash things like keys (that are organized according to different keyrings); odds and ends I pick up but have yet to figure out a place for; and quick pick-ups like gum, breath mints, sunglasses, and my iPod or cell phone.

MONTHLY OR YEARLY CALENDAR

I prefer yearly, but use both. If I cannot see everything clearly marked for the day, week, month and year, I have no idea where I'm going or when. My biggest problem comes when I fail to sync the calendar from my computer to my wall. I have a friend who just prints out her computer's calendar every time she makes a change or adds an event. Maybe that's the best idea, especially if you print on the backsides of old copies, in keeping with the go-green movement.

STORAGE FURNITURE

Shop in specialty stores that serve people in dorms and small apartments for unique furniture that pulls double duty in function. Big bulk items like blankets, pillows, books and anything else you can think of can be stashed away in your storage furniture indefinitely and on a moment's notice.

EXTRA COPIES

I have multiple copies of my favorite reference books, important papers and everyday essentials, like contact lens solution, all-in-one cabinet for the many occasions I lose or misplace the must-haves in my life. When my daughter was in high school, we had doubles of her textbooks and assignments knowing it was just a matter of time before she lost them or forgot an assignment at school.

LISTS

"To-do" lists are a way of life for the organized Aspie. Mine are written on napkins, in little journals I have in my purse, on the back of receipts and on torn-off paper I collect from wherever I see it. Not the best system, but it works for me if I stuff all the various lists I've made into my back pocket where they will be safe and sound until I get home and unload them. I keep them in one big stack, checking off what's been accomplished. The stack is never empty, but only because my lists get added to every day.

VISUAL ADVERTISING

Cut out pictures from a magazine that represent what you need to do and then post them on a spot you can't miss. For example, if you want to clean the floors sometime during your week, find a broom or mop advertisement and stick it up as an obvious visual reminder.

Executive toys

I was at a Tony Attwood conference when I first heard the term "executive toys." Dr. Attwood cleverly pointed out today's PDAs, laptops, calculators, etc. serve a great purpose for helping us with executive functioning that includes reminders and note taking. They have come down in price over the years and simple ones (sometimes simple is better!) are quite inexpensive at toy stores. Use the note-taking functions on your executive toy as both your personal reminder secretary and as a way to remind you of where you stashed your things.

Portable emergency kit

So much of what we do these days requires transporting to and fro between our home, therapy center, school, work, shopping and extra-curricular activities and duties. Sometimes it feels like I spend more time in my car than in an actual building. Keeping an emergency kit in the car filled with things I might need but would normally keep only at home, helps me feel less stressed when I am away from my home base. Consider the following things for your emergency kit, making certain to customize the contents as needed for you. Deodorant, mouthwash, gum, comfortable walking shoes, Band-Aids, disinfectant, instant thermometer, common medications, plastic bags (for trash or in case someone gets car sick), snack bars, individual servings of juice or water, paper and pen, tape, paper clip, tissue or napkins, extra batteries for electronic devices, emergency contact information including information on ASD, a clean shirt and pair of pants, blankets and a flashlight.

Assert your best asset—You
TRUST YOUR INSTINCTS

All too often it is important for a person to be able to triage and set instant priorities between competing problems or needs. As Aspies we are prone to analyzing situations to the nth degree or freaking out in the face of pressure. Try letting your gut tell you what to do. If, for instance, you get a call from work demanding you get back to the office to complete a task you might well be able to do at home, and a call from the school nurse telling you your child has fallen on the playground but is not in need of an emergency room visit or doctor's appointment, ask for all the information you can get and then sit a spell and let your instincts help you decide if you should rush back to the office or the school nurse, or neither. Once you've made your decision, and you are confident you have made the best call given all the information you have, don't second-guess yourself. And if it turns out you made a less-than-perfect decision, do not beat yourself up over it. Life tends to go on in more or less a natural rhythm if we nurture it along the way, so that even a slip-up here and there, won't likely cause permanent damage.

JUST SAY NO

Did you know you can and should often say no to requests from others? I used to be so eager for friends and socializing, I'd be the first person to raise my hand and volunteer my home or my time and energy to any cause that would get me a phone call or girlfriend. Not anymore. My friend Reverend Curry once told me if I always volunteered all the time, I was not letting other people experience the joy of giving. Within that line of reasoning, it feels good to say no. Instead of saying yes to everything, I now say yes to pieces of things that I know I can handle from home if I need to. That way if I have a meltdown or am too frustrated or nervous to go out and about, I can still feel a part of the team, but on my own terms.

If you do say yes to more things than you can handle, cheat. Buy cookie dough at the grocery and bake them like you made them from scratch. Make one-pot meals with a slow cooker you don't have to tend to. Pay a neighbor kid to run errands for you. Have a computer-crazed teenager create things like a website or newsletter you agreed to design. Divide and conquer. That's my motto.

Saying no is just part of the assertion process. Say yes to taking care of yourself. Give yourself the command to rest and rejuvenate. Meditate, craft, read, play an instrument, run around the house spinning and singing—do anything that makes your heart comfortable.

YOU ARE A WHOLE PERSON, NOT INDIVIDUAL PIECES

The idiomatic saying *I wear so many different hats* means a person is taking on a variety of roles and jobs, typically beyond the average. It alludes to headgear worn for different professions and it is very apropos for Aspie females on the spectrum who tend to pretend they are more neurotypical than they truly are or wish to be. It is terribly easy for us to feel fragmented just because we walk between neurotypical and ASD. Just thinking about how fragmented we can become when we also factor in the trials of being a mom, wife, co-worker, friend and individual person means we are wearing way too many hats most of the time. Try not to let the hats you wear weigh you down. If you find you are too segmented and becoming too disjointed, narrow who you are into a tighter package. For example, if being a volunteer at a school function puts you out of your comfort zone, drop that hat and go back to just being a conscientious parent of a child in a school who can call on you as a substitute volunteer.

At the end of the day, you are in charge of what you do and how you do it. Through trial and error, combined with sage advice from as many sources as you need to consider, create an environment that works for you. Your efforts in streamlining and working within your comfort zone will pay off in terms of less anxiety, more accomplishments, happier experiences and more efficient time on task.

Chapter 9

Dance with Your Spirit

Tap in to Grace

i and I
i looked inside of me
valleys of emotion everywhere
i noticed light
love richly tucked between my heart and soul
an adventure into spirit called out that day

come join me it said
embrace me fully
I need not be tucked away
yearning to shine in your eyes
to be your playmate throughout life

I have always been here
I will never leave
I await to see you pierce the veil of fear
walk thru the portal of uncertainty
find my embrace
We will forever dance

—Chris Rials-Seitz

So much of this book is daunting and, at times, downright sad. I'm sorry for that, but this book is about the much too covered-up side of Aspie life. I think, hope and pray the more we crack open and confidently discuss the tough stuff, the less power those powerful bits will have over us. That having been said, we have to face the truth that because we are different from the majority, our reality will likely have more complexity and complication than others'. Fine. Bring it on. You can handle anything when you adapt to the sense that you are a strong female who can challenge the toughest of things with a dignity and grace that will bring your heart peace. Be mindful that it is Aspie normal to catch a break filled with possibilities on some days while on other days there won't be enough covers in the world to hide under. On those days, it will be harder to follow a graceful path to whole wellness. Such is life when you live a life suspended between the two worlds, neurotypical and Asperger.

Our community of experts, people on the spectrum and caregivers, talk a lot about how we can cope, disclose and survive life with Asperger syndrome. We Aspies bring the discussion to a deeper level when we share how important it is to practice introspection; how we are happier when we know and can articulate our real self, our needs, wants and super-fine abilities. Each day we learn more about who we are, how we can and should assert our rights to achieve our dreams, and how we can help the NT world speak our language just as we learn how to speak theirs. All these discussions are incredibly valuable. Yes, we have come such a long way... but we need to push ourselves further. We need to dance with our spirit and tap in to a grace that invites us to accept we are worthy and lovely beings.

The English word "spirit," from Latin *spiritus*, means "breath." Many people on the spectrum quite literally forget to breathe. We catch ourselves holding on to our breath as if once we let it go, something dangerous and dark will become us. How ironic, since not breathing adds to our stress, our discomfort and, in fact, bigger challenges to our ability to think clearly. Beyond the notion of breathing, the concept of "spirit" has taken on many connotations over the centuries. Some connotations lean toward a religious bend as in the Holy Spirit or the soul; some toward a sense of emotion as in *Don't get your spirits down, everything will be OK*; and still other interpretations point to the essence of one's character or personality. My definition of the spirit in this chapter is a mix of our emotions and our character with a bit of the divine tossed in for real depth of meaning. On the whole, when I talk of spirit, I mean to suggest I am trying to find that balance that brings out the best of us so that we may feel the best about who we are and the most positive about how others affect us.

How do we do that? How do we dance with our spirit doing happy twirls, safe dips and confident bows? I have found there are plenty of concrete things to do to start to enjoy the dance with the spirit and I have included those in the support section at the end of this chapter, but before turning to the support section, it's important to think conceptually about how we might reach the spirit. Dancing with the spirit, to me at least, is about getting in touch with the inner voice, it is about the grace of our journey that teaches us not just who we are but who we are meant to be. That inner voice puts us on a spirit quest that goes beyond all limits, asking only that we keep an open mind which will allow us to think beyond the past and on to a present and future state where grace and kindness abound.

To begin with, I try to focus on the good stuff that takes my life from mundane or depressing to worthwhile and good. So in my terms, this means I focus on the things important to me like developing my self-worth, taking care of my pets and people, living according to my sense of morality, spreading kindness in a play-it-forward golden rule kind of way. And guess what? When I am successful at this, my spirit fully charges and I feel a confidence and serenity that makes breathing easier and smiling easiest.

One of the best things about this spirit dance is that it is a solo dance. I don't need anyone around me for any of this. If I'm having a bad-friend day or a day when people seem to be too unsavory, or life too frightening or risky, I can spend time in private meditation sending positive thoughts to those who are unkind, or to those who need help, or just to the world in general. I can ride my horse and disappear into an honest place of mutual trust that transcends pettiness and anger. I can wrap my arms around my dogs and let their open trust of human nature warm my heart. I can open a beloved book and jump into a favorite writer's world as if it were my own. I can sit outside on a park bench and silently talk to the consciousness I believe is universal and a part of every human being until my thoughts go beyond the moment and into things of everlasting importance, until I feel like all my parts and all the parts of everyone and everything else on our planet join in a calm unity

I am unable to articulate. Or I can connect with the things that made me develop the best part of me.

~

I met the first person I knew who had autism in 1962. I was three years old. The little girl's name was Marilyn and she was probably five or six, but she acted more like a baby than I did. She carried around her baby bottle always filled with some sort of drink (a habit I quickly latched on to and carried with me through my early teens for times when I needed extra comfort), and she wore diapers. Marilyn had no speech other than grunting and screaming. Three older brothers helped her parents keep Marilyn from running too far too quickly, as she was indeed a classic bolter. But the neighborhood accepted Marilyn for Marilyn. A special little girl who rode the special school bus who would pop up and scream then pop away to find something else to get on with. Scotty was the brother I played with most. We played all things boys, because I like boy games far better than girl games. Boy games were about strict rules and carried on with very little social finesse. Scott was very nice to me and must have thought me a decent enough playmate because he often chose my friendship over the other kids in the neighborhood.

I wonder now, if Marilyn helped me find Scott. Did her spirit set his free to welcome people who were different? Did Scott see me as just another kid, rather than a kid with an obvious case of Asperger syndrome? And what of the rest of the neighborhood who helped with Marilyn, and even me when I wandered to some rooftop or sewer? Were their spirits warm and open because together we taught each other the real value of humanity in all its many flavors and nuances? I think so. I hope so. The dance with people who have open spirits that nurture and accept is my favorite spirit dance.

I realize hindsight can take away some of the bitter glare of my past, but I don't think it has re-colored these memories. I ask my best friend Maureen and her siblings and my mother all about our old days and every one of them confirms we were who we were, and we were better off from having known each other.

~

Even though my memories are as accurate as memories can be, I do believe I am finally learning to put in more optimism where harmful memories try to muck around. A certain amount of optimism is essential for the spirit dance to work. Toward that feeling of hope, I believe when we can shake off the bad stuff and see ourselves as creatively and divinely inspired wondrous creatures with an infinite capacity for love and purpose, with the ability to forgive others and ourselves, we can start connecting with our true beauty and the beauty in others. Put another way, when we can see beyond the ugliness and the bullying, the pitfalls and the harsh parts of our everyday lives, we can start to see the good stuff that is there if we will only reach out and accept it, rejecting the bad that would tie us to a life of conflict and strife. When we think positively we begin to dance and when we let our spirit take the lead, we have the power to reject negativity and accept only those things that fill our life with promise and dignity.

It is so cool to welcome the spirit, to trust that we can affect it and enjoy this part of our connection to self and others. When we dance with our spirit, we embrace the notion of going forward, of looking for true purpose and direction far beyond what others tell us we should or can't, will or won't, be able to do. We toss off the arguments, the school or workplace conferences that restrict our worth to whether or not we are behaving according to code or managing to keep our differences well hidden and in check. We open our heart and our soul and our mind, inviting all three to connect and swirl. We find our pulse point and wake up each morning feeling blessed by whomever or whatever, for simply having yet another day to explore our world and make our life count for something. That's a lot of dancin'!

I believe when we treat our spirit as a treasure, it will heal all that ails. For example, I am now able to forgive. It took me decades to learn the importance of forgiveness. On one level it means little to forgive, but on the level of the spirit, it means so very much. It can literally mean the difference between good health and bad. Research shows that when we hold on to bitter thoughts or too much anger and fear toward past memories or toward the people and pain in our lives, our body creates too much of the hormone cortisol, which can lead to autoimmune disease, heart disease and impaired memory; three issues I am currently living with, but devoted to eradicating. All that devastation, for what? Does the anger and frustration we harbor toward the assaults on our body help us? Does it even the score? Does it make us better people, happier, more well adjusted? Nope. The best way to get over the negative crap we've had tossed in our path is to jump over and ahead of it all, reaching for our spirit to lift us and take us to places we might never have known existed if we hadn't tried in earnest to reach them and rest within them.

I think this book is about many themes beyond the obvious literal theme of staying safe. Safety at its core is about staying alive. But that is not enough. We deserve so much more than waking up each day with dread in our heart or fear in our soul. We deserve a life that is grounded in good things and happiness, and we can refuse to let anyone or anything take that right from us. Yes, we will all go through rock-bottom gut-wrenching stuff that nearly does us in, but it is up to us to make the choice to go inward and find the spirit that will bring us to the safe places where we can rest well far beyond the bad yesterdays or iffy tomorrows.

You are ultimately in control of your tranquility and life's joy. Dance with your spirit and smile.

"A graceful dance" supports

The spirit dance has been choreographed into countless renditions throughout time. Religious, cultural, generational and even gender influences have played a very significant role in how, when and why the spirit should move. It seems to me that nowadays there is a lively and lovely blend of all sorts of ideas when even the mere idea of the spirit is entertained. For this chapter I decided to leave the precise definition of spirit to my readers, and instead suggest some ideas on how to open that place in your world where all kinds of spirit notions can stir. That having been said, the following questions are meant to tweak your vision of your spirit. I hope they help you dance.

Questions to get your spirit stirring

- What are the big life questions I think I need to ponder most?
- Am I happy in my life right now?
- Why am I happy or unhappy?
- Do I have people in my life I feel I can share my most personal thoughts and stories with?
- What might happen once I share my personal information?
- How do the people in my life affect my daily living and goals?

- What are my dreams and goals?

- If money were not an issue, what would my dream job be?

- Where would I like to be in one year? five years? ten years? twenty?

- Is life preordained or do we have free will?

- What defines a good person?

- To what do we owe nature and animals?

- How can I help those people and things I believe need help?

- Is life supposed to be lived without strife or challenges?

As you begin to form the answers to the questions that surround a life based on the spiritual questions, try to find people to share the questions with. Good, open discussions can do much to set the Aspie mind gently at ease. We are opinionated people who not only deserve a right to our opinions, but a place to say them without worrying about permanent negative repercussions.

Contemplate

Asking and discussing the big questions can be pushed to an even higher level when we record them for additional and continued contemplation. Few questions can be answered adequately once and for all at any time. Every day we learn more things, and new things that can alter our perception and set our spirit into new directions. To keep track of my big questions and conceivable answers I:

- *Keep a journal.* Special moments, experiences, events, thoughts and deeds, both the good and the harrowing, are kept in my journals. When I read my old words of wisdom, I never fail to learn more about myself or the issue at hand. My journals help me remember who I was when, how I am now, and who I wish to be tomorrow. It's like reading a history book and speaking to a fortuneteller at the same time. Very inspiring for the spirit.

- *Write gratitudes.* I write myself notes about what I'm thankful for. They may be little things, like I am grateful I am a brunette who tans easily, to big things, like I am grateful I have healthy children. No gratitude goes without my acknowledgment and every good thing counts as a blessing in my book. When I see how many blessings I have, my spirit is happy.

Serve

Service is very good for the spirit. It is true it can be better to give than to receive, and I find when I'm helping others it is hard to concentrate on my own issues. I get very into the mode of being present for people who need anything I can offer. If you feel so inclined, do consider community service, as it will help you see how you fit in with a world beyond ASD and beyond your own space. As an extra bonus, when we volunteer we tend not to be seen as people with differences, but as people who care. That can't be anything but positive for all involved, the spirit included!

Inspire

It would be awesome if we could all travel the world looking for reams of experience and self-enlightenment, but this is surely impossible for most of us. As a decent alternative, surround your environment and soul with the things that make you think on an intuitive level, or at least a level that furthers your self-knowledge and world experience.

Forgiveness

Aspies' tenacious and often single-minded outlook can make forgiveness extremely difficult to imagine, much less accomplish. Even though I know it is essential to forgive the many people in my life who set traps for my vulnerability or who hurt my pride or person, I seem unable to get very far. If I do manage to forgive people for harming me in one way or another, I seem totally unable even to contemplate forgiving people for harming others, especially the innocent youth, elderly and special. I understand the concept of undoing the dam that a heart full of anger will create. I know harboring anger or distrust keeps me from moving forward in my spiritual journey, but without logic to explain to me why someone hurt me (or someone else), I am unarmed to knock my dismay out of the way. These are the things I contemplate, hoping the logic behind the sentiments will teach me how to forgive.

- Studies show people are happier and healthier when they can forgive.

- My past is what made me who I am.

- If I let the things that have happened to me continue to plague my mind, they will imprison me in their nasty world.

- Love. Just love.

- Forgive in pieces. One tiny thing first, then another, then another, until the whole lump of nastiness is wiped clean away.

Have forgiveness parties just for you. I reward myself with something cool when I do manage to put the bad away for good. The reward might be something tangible, a special dessert or a message I write myself to express I completed a job well done. The point isn't the reward, but the fact I accomplished a very difficult task.

Forgiveness does not mean forgetting or accepting. To me, it means saying a farewell to the anger and pain caused by that which I forgive.

Learn from the philosophers

Deep thinkers have long been sharing stirring thoughts of the spirit. Think on these quotes:

> *Though the path is plain and smooth for men of good will, he who walks it will not travel far, and will do so only with difficulty, if he does not have good feet: that is, courage and a persevering spirit.*
> —St. John of the Cross

> *Give me a spirit that on this life's rough sea / Loves to have his sails filled with a lusty wind, / Even till his sail-yards tremble, his masts crack, / And his rapt ship run on her side so low / That she drinks water, and her keel ploughs air.*
> —George Chapman

> *Man learns through experience, and the spiritual path is full of different kinds of experiences. He will encounter many difficulties and obstacles, and they are the very experiences he needs to encourage and complete the cleansing process.*
> —Yogi Sai Baba

> *The fruit of the Spirit is love, joy, peace, patience, kindness, goodness, faithfulness, gentleness and self-control.*
> —The Bible

Sitting with these words and digging further into their essence, I find peace and real hope in their insights. They tell us our spirit can guide us to the light at the end of the proverbial tunnel. They tell us our spirit bears with it good things we may all have access to. They tell us the pain and ugliness we have had tossed both literally and figuratively at our being, are things we can use as stepping stones toward a higher understanding of what in the heck this life might just be about. Instead of letting the nasty things we have encountered represent rocks that tear our flesh off and grind our spirit to dust, isn't it far cooler to picture those rocks as boulders we can stack one on top of the other until they are stepping stones we can climb on in our journey toward seeing far and beyond the pettiness and cruelty? To me it is far more interesting and appealing to view the pain of the past as tools that can ultimately set us on a course of illumination and heightened spirituality.

The ancient arts

Exercise heals the mind and not just because it creates serotonin, the happiness hormone. I discussed the importance of exercise and meditation in the Mood Marauders chapter, but they should be repeated here. Steeping oneself in the ancient traditions like yoga, tai chi, qigong, martial arts, prayer and meditation makes me connect with the centuries and centuries of those who have gone before us. When I engage in things I know other people have turned to for a spirit high, I feel my own spiritual awakening getting higher. So high, in fact, it can be daunting. Have no fear though, when you connect with that place in your spirit that can so easily remain hidden unless you focus long and hard on letting it shine, the feeling of peace and tranquility you will feel is undeniably sweet and well worth any initial hesitation you may have felt when you first tapped in to a deeper consciousness.

Animals

Animal therapy is sprinkled all over this book, as well, but I'm taking it a bit further here. Remembering that the rewards of pet therapy are undeniable, I always wonder if the countries that have more lenient policies toward pets in public places have a lowered degree of public angst. I think they must! For those of us who love them, pets are the best anti-anxiety and heart healers available, and they are Aspies' kindred spirits. Temple Grandin talks about this in her fabulous book *Animals in Translation*. Animals and people on the spectrum have an undeniable connection, especially if the autistic loves animals. I can quite literally feel my horse change the way he moves, depending on how I feel. When

I feel feisty, he matches my energy. When I am low, he quits eating his hay to nudge me. No matter how I feel, I spend time grooming my horse. It never ceases to amaze me how fine this simple act is. A soft curry down the horse's back warms my muscles and my heart; a stirring combination that is tremendously powerful.

My dog, too, knows when I'm out of sync or when I want to play. The moment a tear falls, my dog comes to my rescue to sit by me. This may not sound like a big deal, but this particular dog is not a cuddler. The attention she gives just when I need it proves to me she understands her human is in some sort of strife. Animals can sense danger and happiness, big emotions, the important emotions. They run to the hills when a flood is coming, to the barn when a storm is on the horizon, toward helpful hands and away from evil. It is basic survival skills 101. A trait I think people with an ASD share alongside their animal friends.

I like thinking I am animal-like. It reminds me to open my other voice, the sixth sense if you will. I believe Aspies have a sixth sense that lets them tune into something that compensates for our lack of social sense. Sort of like a blind person tends to have better than average hearing to help them compensate for a lost sense. Every time I hear my gut telling me something, I try to listen. Years of experience have taught me that when I ignore even the quiet whispers of my inner voice, I will live to regret it. Until I believed in my sixth sense, I would ignore the whisper telling me to run, or scream, or ferret away from an abuser or awful situation, but when I learned to tune in and respect the sixth sense, my painful situations were avoided more often. It's such a powerful feeling to know that while I may lack the neurotypical sense of the word "social," I can tap into a vision and sensory experience that few others can.

Surround yourself with your favorite things

Nature = nurture for me. I like to look out my window and see at least a patch of green and a clump of leaves. When it is impossible for me to see the real thing, I look at nature scenes on my computer screen. Hotels and spas realize the gentle calm our scenery brings us and many now offer small plants or even goldfish you can borrow during your stay at their location. Anything that tickles your soul or brings you to a place of peace and happiness is just plain old good for the spirit. I know folks who like to collect all sorts of things from their travels. Things like photographs, folk art, kaleidoscopes, marbles, first edition books, soap stone carvings and sewing thimbles. I also know people who collect animal bones sculptures, gum wrappers and notebooks. What we collect isn't as important as the sheer thrill of collecting and the sheer comfort the items bring us. We are Aspies who might collect just about anything. I like that. The more interesting the collection, the happier it makes me feel. But I have to advise that you don't let your collection become an obsession to the point of hoarding or stress if you can't find or keep something you really love. The collecting is supposed to give your spirit a tweak that makes it play, not a punch in the gut that makes it lame. And while you are collecting, don't be surprised if you meet other collectors who share a similar interest in your favorite things. New friends can be found among fellow collectors.

Pray

Pray to your higher power if you are a believer, to yourself, or to the entity who you feel answers your heart-felt hopes and notions. In other words, send out special thoughts directed toward the energy that answers your call. Prayer can be about anything and it can be made at anytime in any way. For a few ideas you might consider praying to give thanks; to ask for something, such as fortitude or personal growth; for release from pain or unease; for forgiveness of others and for yourself if you are having a tough time letting go of any past mistakes; and for guidance in making decisions or for help in assessing situations.

Live in grace

I love the word *grace*. It has so many lovely connotations with no negative stigmas attached. You can use it to give praise for a behavior, such as *She exuded grace during this uncomfortably awkward situation*. Or to expresses a beauty or something fine to behold, for example *She dances with effortless grace*. It also means something is good when it is used in virtually anything social, for to have good graces means you are polite and pleasant. Above all these, my favorite connotation for the word *grace* is a spiritual one. As a Christian, when I think of grace, I think more of my relationship to God, which reflects my belief that God is a gracious creator who welcomes everyone into his love. This belief brings me comfort, especially when I feel unloved or disliked by others who think of my AS as a challenge they cannot handle.

No matter how you use the word *grace*, when you hear it, I hope you let it remind you of good things and let it bring you to the thought that you are worthy of a life with lots of grace in it, even if for you that simply means being considered a person who has a kind spirit. But as for me, I will go a bit further and let the word infuse me with all it can mean, especially when it comes to my religious beliefs. This poem by my dear friend the Reverend Richard Curry finds its way into my meditation and prayers often. I like it because it beseeches all of us to believe we are all valuable people.

> *Grace*
> *Freely, willingly giving*
> *Receiving without deserving*
> *Completes the circle of loving*
> *Capstone of life worth living.*

Energize

I was fortunate to have a professor of movement science on my dissertation committee. She taught me how important movement is to living well, healthy and balanced. In school we aren't reminded of these things. Instead, we tend to be taught team sports and competitions are the most important aspects of physical education. This is an unfortunately one-sided message. To begin with, it reduces exercise to something rather superficial and superfluous, and for an Aspie it makes the point of exercise non-applicable simply because we aren't big team joiners and our bilateral communication and sensory issues make real competing in sports unobtainable for most of us. Movement science professors, occupational and physical therapists, exercise coaches, natural movement masters, martial arts instructors, holistic healers and every health professional worth a grain of salt can tell you movement is as essential to your bones and muscles, balance and flexibility, as it is to the mind/body connection. Movement brings good energy into our lives, and in so doing it wakes the spirit to good things. You may not consider yourself a competitor or a great athlete and that is more than fine. When you think about moving your body to find that sense of energy and connection I'm talking about here, go outside the box and consider the following physical experiences as adventures you might like to learn or do more often.

EXERCISE ON THE GROUND

Walk or hike. The only thing you need when you walk is your two feet, a few safety precaution items and some common sense planning.

- Bring lots of water and a healthy snack for replenishment and to keep your energy and blood sugar level.

- In addition to your cell phone (which may not get a signal on a hike in the wilderness), bring bells or a loud whistle to alert help should you get hurt or lost.

- Bring a first-aid kit with all the basics and items of need that are particular to your hiking area; for example, cortisone, should you think you will encounter poisonous plants or stinging insects.

- Take clothes to match the weather and potential weather changes.

- Be aware of the area's wildlife and learn how to deal with them should you run into something dangerous.

- Do not wander from the marked trails.

- Let someone know where you will be hiking.

- Carry your important emergency medical and contact information with you.

- Hike with a companion or group if possible, especially when you are trying out a new trail.

STEP IT UP A NOTCH

Ask any runner and they will tell you a bit of speed behind a walk increases their energy, their brainpower and their happiness quotient. If you have healthy feet, ankles and knees, take your walk to the next level and see if the freedom that comes from a brisk move through the world makes your spirit happier.

Some ideas: speed walk; jog; run; commit to a marathon on behalf of a charity; mix up a run with a bit of walking, jogging and a short burst of speed. (Note—don't go a major distance or up your speed until your body is ready to do so.)

GET IN THE WATER

When I was a kid, swimming saved my spirit. I would spend hours swimming in circles, jumping up and down in the shallow part of a pool and just floating. The sensation of my weightless body was as calming to me as a warm blanket is to a puppy missing his mates. Water therapy is a real soother, and it is widely seen as a great way to help people on the spectrum improve range of motion, balance and sensory integration; learn mobility skills; and experience additional neuro-development. If you can't swim, either learn how or, if you have a lifeguard present, put on a life vest and float your way through the water, letting the rhythm of the motion soothe your soul.

CANOE/SAIL/PADDLEBOAT THROUGH IT

My mom and I spent lots of afternoons exploring one of the small lakes at the St. Louis zoo by way of a paddleboat. The combination of real exertion mixed with the serenity of the water and beauty of the birds and wildlife sharing our exploration was almost tangibly relaxing and spirit soothing. I highly recommend any kind of boat experience that taxes your heart rate and muscles while providing you with a serene view.

Be active on the ice and and in the snow

If calorie burning is an indication of an activity worth your while, downhill and cross-country skiing, snowboarding, and ice-skating are more than worth your time. But more important than the calories they burn is the opportunity these activities give you to see the world in slow motion, in suspended animation. Because Aspies can often take quite cold weather without much of a fuss we can take part in the frozen outdoors with excitement and curiosity that is only matched by the special way nature shines in the snow. There is a special quiet when it is super cold, the kind of quiet that serves sensory-overloaded people very well. Moving among the quiet cold is tremendously rewarding. If you are not coordinated enough or interested enough in the big ice and snow activities, try old-fashioned energy builders like building igloos and snowmen or snow shoe walking or ice fishing—anything that lets your spirit calm down and breathe, just breathe.

Cave hunt

Caves are vast openings that afford their visitors a feeling of spacious openness with almost perfect acoustics and sensory conditions, or cozy nuggets that provide a feeling of closed-in comfort. As a kid I was infamous for climbing down into or right through any small opening I could find. Since I am a Missouri native, caves were everywhere for me to go visit; something I did repeatedly with my schoolmates and later with my own children just for fun. My husband and I explored a cave on our honeymoon. I highly recommend a trip to a cave if you can find the opportunity. However, unless you are a professional caver, you need to go with a group even if it makes you socially uncomfortable. Take solace in the fact people on field trips are more interested in the trip than in your personality, so don't let anxiety or social awkwardness interfere with your desire to check out a cool cave.

Hug a tree

You might not be able to go climbing in a cave, but chances are good you can find a tree to climb, swing from or sit under. Parks are in most areas and loads of people are lucky enough to have a tree or two in their own yard. I like trees so much, I'd keep a naked Christmas tree up all year if I couldn't find a real one, and beneath it I would sit on a blanket as if I was in the outdoors having a real picnic. I had a favorite maple tree right outside my window when I was growing up that kept me company during many long afternoons when I would sit in her arms and wish I could fly. Silly imagination, but so real when up in a tree.

Trees are magnanimous in their capacity to provide for us and stoic in their ability to weather most storms. We could take a lesson or two from them on how to create a spirit that grows with dignity.

Rock climbing and repelling

You absolutely have to get a trained professional to help you learn how to rock climb or repel, but after you do just think of the trips you can take with a partner—the kind that will open your spirit up to wild adventure with an adrenalin rush that will surely make your spirit leap.

Dig

I come from a long line of farmers and I own a small farm myself. My mother, my father and his father before him taught me how important it is to tend the earth, even though I'm lousy at it. I don't plant a pretty veggie garden, but there is nothing prettier than the hint of every vegetable popping itself through the dirt. I'm better with flowers, and there is nothing quite as cool as the first peek of a perennial. They are such faithful friends that reward again and again for all the hard work we put into them.

Immerse in nature

Many native cultures believe there is a spirit that resides in nature. No matter your religious views, there is no doubt that nature speaks to people in comforting ways. We turn to the land to feed us and to trees to house us. We return people to the ground when they have passed away. We hear a bird chirp or see a new butterfly and are reminded of times when we were happy, or we think spring is on the way and that makes us feel good just thinking about it. There is power in nature no matter what role you give it in your religion, so spend time looking at it—really truly looking at it. Watch the clouds. Gaze at the stars. Sit by the window when a storm is brewing. Stand in the rain. Fluff up the snow. Make mud pies. Cup fresh herbs to your face. Go outside after grass has just been cut. Take in the flowers that come in the summer. Literally let nature envelop you in the ways you enjoy and when it does, it will take your spirit to a natural place of light and reassurance. Of peace.

Appreciate the arts

I have a big coffee table book that features costumes made from real pieces of nature that are meant to fit a fairy. It's a whimsical book, but also a very beautiful display of fine craftsmanship and perfect design. The book entertains me and it lets me go to a different place in my mind when I am with it. I know there are no such things as fairies, but when I have this book in my hand, I can immerse myself in the costume designs and the stories that go with each, and presto—I'm no longer sad or aggravated or agitated. I'm in fairyland with a wide-open spirit awing with delight.

Surround yourself with big coffee table books and do one step beyond that... Go to art galleries, concerts, the theater, films, exhibits of all kinds and you will soon believe there is a growing of the spirit that happens when you surround yourself with beautiful and thought-provoking elements.

Create

I am the first to admit I am not very good at art or craft, but I love making necklaces from beads. There is something really interesting that happens to my sense of spirit when I create something unique from a little bead and some thread. It makes me feel creative. And when I feel creative, I feel I can do anything I like to do better. I feel spirit rich. Give your creativity a try. Grab a camera; a paint brush; a volunteer position at the community theater; a strand of beads and some thread; clay; a musical instrument; or the ingredients for a new recipe and work your way through the creative process that can help you feel a new sense of spirit and adventure, of accomplishment and satisfaction.

Chapter 10
Red Flag Warnings
Or Could This Female Have AS?

And so I wonder as I go,
What are the whys before me now?
Am I unglued when I think of them?
Will the me I want to see be let loose or kept caged?
Is this what life is meant to be?
No.
I think I get to decide.
Life is for me what I want it to be and what I want it to be is real.

—Liane Holliday Willey

There are several professional criteria designed to measure whether or not a person has an ASD. Yet females remain largely underrepresented in these measurement tools. Until our researchers and institutes of higher education decide females really are on the spectrum in numbers far larger than they recognize, it will be up to us, the laypeople, to identify and support our girls and women. Even if a formal diagnosis is never made, I would set up a program of ASD intervention and support as an insurance policy, if nothing else. After all, there really isn't anything in the ASD curriculum that would hurt anyone. Which makes me wonder, why don't we add more ASD friendly supports in every school and system we have? When I was in elementary school, we did. We were directly taught Robert's Rules of Order, acceptable etiquette for a variety of situations, consequences and rewards, and the value of trying our best no matter the ultimate grade or place on the ladder. Our lives were more routine-oriented, less chaotic and far simpler, particularly when it came to sensory overload. We played in groups, all alone, with our animals, out in nature, on a variety of activities that supported our sensory needs, and with invisible friends. I feel like today's world has taken away many of the natural supports we had back before TV and computers took our attention and all of our interest. I love my TV and my computer more than most people, but growing up I think it was ultimately better for me to explore my sensory needs on a daily basis. Digging in dirt and making mud pies was perfect for a sensory seeker. Laying my ice cold back on a hot wall of bricks made my body feel like it fit in space. Riding my horse and swimming were perfect body awareness and bilateral coordination learning experiences. In Girl Scouts we learned about dealing with small groups and the value of independence and the importance of treating one another with respect even if we disliked the person. We did not estimate in our math class, we learned there was a right and wrong answer in math, just as there was a right and wrong answer in grammar and spelling. While I wish we had had some of the executive toys of today, back when I was a kid, we used paper and calendars to organize our schedules, and bulletin boards to provide us with images we could learn from. And we took plenty of field trips to build our schema and make us more comfortable in the world of the unknown so that we could ultimately do more to predict what we might be getting into; such an important element of success for people like me. Neighbors watched neighbors, older kids looked after younger kids, and despite the inevitable cliques and groups, people took more time to get to know other people so that at least a *Hello* and a *Have a good day* were exchanged. Good old-fashioned social skills, everyone could learn.

Ah. I sound like an old lady, and maybe I always was. My point is, with or without a diagnosis, we in society can do much more to recognize and support people with differences. We used to do it better on many levels. If we could combine the old-school positive practices with the new-school understanding and advancements in therapy, medication and instructional designs, maybe, just maybe, we would have an even better way to make life for everyone on the spectrum more fruitful and happy.

Traits to look for

Diagnosis or not, the indicators below are warning signs that the brain is mismatching signals. A trip to the physical or occupational therapist, developmental pediatrician, cognitive behavioral specialist, autism specialist or someone well versed in ASD would be in order if you see a female exhibiting more than a few of these traits. While autism in its purest form is often easy enough to diagnose, people, especially females, will need to have their ASD teased out. A good specialist will know how to serve as a detective finding the ASD traits hidden behind a mask of pretending or by excellent echolalia skills and compensation strategies. These are the signs to watch for:

- Walks on the tippy toes.
- Walks into walls.
- Stomps like she is wearing Frankenstein shoes, loud and forceful.
- Unable to figure out personal space. Gets too close or stands too far away.
- Poor eye/hand coordination. Simple tasks like tying a shoe or braiding hair may be nearly impossible.
- Odd large motor coordination. Throwing a ball and skipping may be very difficult if not impossible.
- Pulls on hair. Pulls hair (or eyebrows or eyelashes) out. Chews hair. Knots hair. Won't allow hair to be brushed and/or washed.
- Very picky eater who might actually throw up at the smell of a food, or tantrum when a food she doesn't like is brought to the table.
- Describes beverages as too thick, gooey or some other odd adjective.
- Shows an eating disorder might develop.
- Constant stomachaches and headaches, and irritable bowel syndrome could occur.
- Covers ears at sudden or loud noises.
- Flaps, turns circles, and acts out in odd ways when stressed by too many visual or auditory distractions.
- Vomits or complains at certain smells.
- Touches and squishes everything she sees from cracks in mud to jellyfish.

- Refuses to touch or go near almost everything in the environment from silk fabrics to craft dough.

- Wears shoes, belts, scarves and other accessories as tight as handcuffs on a prisoner.

- Refuses to wear anything tight.

- Talks in one big monologue.

- Shows signs of an above-average vocabulary at an early age.

- Reads at an early age, though when a comprehension test is given it becomes clear the child is word calling, having memorized the words without realizing what the sentences mean and the story is saying.

- Speech may sound like a robot or brilliant professor giving a lecture without much change in speech rate or pitch and tone.

- Interrupts people when they are talking.

- Walks away in the middle of a conversation as if it is the perfectly normal thing to do.

- Resists talking, but points, grunts or draws to show you what she wants.

- Shares infrequently.

- Receives few invitations to be with other children.

- Plays with animals more often than other children or people.

- Has few friendships or only one friend at a time.

- Shows extreme sensitivity to teasing.

- Shows ill temper or illness at parties, theme parks and other large-group activities.

- Plays with imaginary friends and in pretend worlds only she can see.

- Plays pretend in an odd way. For instance, dolls are arranged by size or hair color. Favorite things get displayed on a shelf in a certain way and are not played with in traditional ways. Large collections are categorized. Groups of toy birds are put into biological classes.

- Illustrates poor handwriting. Cursive might be particularly difficult. Words might not have spaces between them. Sentences will often lean upwards or downwards, but rarely straight across unlined paper.

- Can't hold the writing tools correctly, holding them too hard and almost like one would hold a knife they are ready to slice into a watermelon.

- Insists on wearing only one piece of favored clothing.

- Can't wear clothes with tags and other scratchy things in the seams.

- Misunderstands jokes, sarcasm, innuendos and double meanings.

- Doesn't comprehend beyond the very literal.

- May laugh at the wrong thing or laugh at the wrong time, for example, at a funeral or during a religious service.

- May not know the meaning of walking a mile in someone else's shoes. Empathy and understanding may never occur, at least not naturally.

- Talks too bluntly.

- Has narrow and deep and, sometimes, all-encompassing interests.

- Makes poor eye contact or will be piercing like a wolf on his prey.

- Has an excellent memory, particularly visual memory. Tends to think in pictures.

- Shows splinter skills, where some talents are super high on the achievement chart and others are very low.

- Melts down when there is a change in a routine.

Is it important to have a diagnosis if the individual is doing well enough without one? I don't really have the answer to that question, but I do believe you don't have to have a diagnosis to take advantage of any learning tools you can find and apply. It is very important to remember that many adults learn how to hide their challenges exceptionally well. But I like to think they shouldn't—at the end of the day the exhaustion levels and stress from doing so can be debilitating. In my opinion, everyone should know how to use her Asperger syndrome as a gift that enriches without exhausting. AS will never go away; the first step is recognizing you have an issue, recognizing that you are not broken but otherwise fixed. When you do, you will be your best advocate and protector. Go, girls, go!

Resources and Recommended Reading

Online resources by chapter

Chapter 1 Healthy Relationships, Safe Socializing: Staying Safe and Well

Women's Health
www.womenshealth.gov

Chapter 2 Falling Prey: But Not Falling Forever

Bullying
www.bullying.org

Bullying Statistics
www.bullyingstatistics.org

Chapter 3 *Broken Bonds: For When Something or Someone You Love Is Lost Forever*

The Association for Death Education and Counseling
www.adec.org

The Shiva Foundation
http://goodgrief.org

The Rainbows Bridge (for pet bereavement)
http://rainbowsbridge.com

Chapter 4 *Mood Mauraders: Or How to Ruin a Perfectly Good Day*

National Association of Cognitive-Behavioral Therapists
www.nacbt.org

American Psychological Association
www.apa.org

The Association for Applied Psychophysiology and Biofeedback
www.aapb.org

U.S. National Institutes of Health
www.nih.gov

Chapter 5 *Out and About: Or Traveling To and Fro*

Journeywoman
www.journeywoman.com

Transportation Security Administration
www.tsa.gov

Women Travel the World
www.womentravelblog.com

Chapter 6 Body Beware: Keeping the Mind and Body Connected

Brain Physics: OCD, Anxiety, Eating Disorders and Impulse Control
www.brainphysics.com

The Dyspraxia Foundation
www.dyspraxiafoundation.org.uk

Irlen Lenses
http://irlen.com

National Eating Disorders Association
www.nationaleatingdisorders.org

Sensory Processing Disorder Resource Center
www.sensory-processing-disorder.com

Vestibular Disorders Association
www.vestibular.org

Chapter 7 What's Looks Got to Do with It? More Than I Like to Admit

Dress for Success
www.dressforsuccess.org

Chapter 8 Living the Life Easy? Juggling Life vs. the Urge to Run Away

Women's Creative Life Link (I also like this blog for all things female)
www.womenslifelink.com

Chapter 9 *Dance with Your Spirit: Tap in to Grace*

Yoga Journal
www.yogajournal.com

The Qigong Institute
www.qigonginstitute.org

American Horticultural Therapy Association
www.ahta.org

Art and the Spirit: Prayer, Healing and Personal Growth Through Line and Color
www.artandthespirit.com

Experts and groups

Assistance Dogs of America Incorporated
www.adai.org

Behavioral Resources and Institute for Neuropsychological Services (B.R.A.I.N.S.)
www.brainspotential.com

Annette Harkness
www.aspiegrrl.wordpress.com

Professional Education and Respite Service
www.vacationrespite.com

The Online Asperger Syndrome Information and Support (OASIS) with MAAP Services for Autism and Asperger Syndrome
www.aspergersyndrome.org

The College Internship Program at the Brevard Center
www.brevardcenter.org

Tony Attwood, Ph.D.
www.tonyattwood.com.au

Autism Women's Network
http://autismwomensnetwork.org

Autistic Self Advocacy Network
www.autisticadvocacy.org

Au-Some Women and Girls Support Group (on Facebook)
www.facebook.com/pages/Au-Some-Women-and-Girls
/163376830352181

National Autistic Society
www.autism.org.uk

Dennis Debbaudt
www.autismriskmanagement.com

Isabelle Hénault, Ph.D.
www.rcaas.org/henault.html

Liane Holliday Willey, EdD
www.aspie.com

Shana Nichols, Ph.D.
www.aspirecenterforlearning.com

Johnny Seitz and Chris Rials-Seits
www.biotyping.com

Stephen Shore, EdD
www.autismasperger.net

Rudy Simone
www.help4aspergers.com

National Health Service—Living with Autism
www.nhs.uk/Livewell/Autism

Other books of interest by Jessica Kingsley Publishers

22 Things a Woman Must Know
If She Loves a Man with Asperger's Syndrome
Rudy Simone
Foreword by Maxine Aston

All Cats Have Asperger Syndrome
Kathy Hoopmann

Asperger Syndrome and Long-Term Relationships
Ashley Stanford
Foreword by Liane Holliday Willey

Asperger's Syndrome and Sexuality: From Adolescence through Adulthood
Isabelle Hénault
Foreword by Tony Attwood

Aspergirls
Empowering Females with Asperger Syndrome
Rudy Simone
Foreword by Liane Holliday Willey

Authentic Movement: Moving the Body, Moving the Self, Being Moved.
A Collection of Essaysc – Volume Two
Edited by Patrizia Pallaro

Autism, Advocates, and Law Enforcement Professionals
Recognizing and Reducing Risk Situations for People with Autism Spectrum Disorders
Dennis Debbaudt

Bully Blocking
Six Secrets to Help Children Deal with Teasing and Bullying (Revised edition)
Evelyn M. Field

Chi for Children
A Practical Guide to Teaching Tai Chi and Qigong in Schools and the Community
Betty Sutherland

The Complete Guide to Asperger's Syndrome
Tony Attwood

The Expressive Body in Life, Art and Therapy
Working with Movement, Metaphor and Meaning
Daria Halprin
Foreword by Jack S. Weller

The Girl Who Spoke with Pictures
Autism Through Art
Eileen Miller
Foreword by Robert Nickel MD
Illustrated by Kim Miller

Girls Growing Up on the Autism Spectrum
What Parents and Professionals Should Know About the Pre-Teen and Teenage Years
Shana Nichols
With Gina Marie Moravcik and Samara Pulver Tetenbaum

Grief in Children
A Handbook for Adults (2nd edition)
Atle Dyregrov
Foreword by Professor William Yule

Inside Anorexia
The Experiences of Girls and their Families
Christine Halse, Anne Honey and Desiree Boughtwood

Let's Talk Relationships
Activities for Exploring Love, Sex, Friendship and Family with Young People
Vanessa Rogers

Making Sense of Sex
A Forthright Guide to Puberty, Sex and Relationships for People with Asperger's Syndrome
Sarah Attwood
Illustrated by Jonathon Powell

Mind/Body Techniques for Asperger's Syndrome
The Way of the Pathfinder
Ron Rubio
Forewords by Irene Brody and Anthony Castrogiovanni

Parenting Girls
Janet Irwin, Susanna de Vries and Susan Stratigos Wilson

The People in a Girl's Life
How to Find Them, Better Understand Them and Keep Them
Martha Kate Downey and Kate Noelle Downey

Sexuality and Women with Learning Disabilities
Michelle McCarthy
Foreword by Hilary Brown

Still Here with Me
Teenagers and Children on Losing a Parent
Edited by Suzanne Sjöqvist
Translated by Margaret Myers

Using Expressive Arts to Work with Mind, Body and Emotions
Theory and Practice
Mark Pearson and Helen Wilson

Vital Healing
Energy, Mind and Spirit in Traditional Medicines of India, Tibet and the
Middle East – Middle Asia
Marc S. Micozzi
With Donald McCown, Mones Abu-Asab, Hakima Amri, Kevin Ergil, Howard Hall, Hari Sharma and Kenneth G. Zysk

Working with Young Women
Activities for Exploring Personal, Social and Emotional Issues
2nd edition
Vanessa Rogers

Yoga for Children with Autism Spectrum Disorders
A Step-by-Step Guide for Parents and Caregivers
Dion E. Betts and Stacey W. Betts
Forewords by Louise Goldberg, Registered Yoga Teacher, and Joshua S. Betts